Christina Reeves

Dimitrios Spanos

THE
MIND
IS THE
MAP

————— WORKBOOK —————

*Awareness is the Compass, and Emotional Intelligence
is the Key to Living Mindfully from the Heart*

The Mind is the Map Workbook

By Dimitrios Spanos and Christina Reeves

1. <PSYCHOLOGY / Emotions> 2. <BODY, MIND & SPIRIT / Inspiration & Personal

Growth> 3. <SELF-HELP / Personal Growth / Success >

Copyright number TX8681925

Workbook ISBN: 978-1-7322054-4-4

Library of Congress Control Number: pending

Cover design by https://damonza.com

Edited by: https://damonza.com

Graphics, illustrations and design layout by : Isabella Hinojal

Printed in the United States of America

Publisher: Eudaimonia Center LLC

23-31 37th Street, Astoria, N.Y 11105

718-397-0290

https://themindisthemap.com

Table of Contents

THE MIND IS THE MAP

WORKBOOK

THIS WORKBOOK PROVIDES the supplemental material, directly from and related to our book, *The Mind is the Map*. The text provided in this workbook covers the self-help exercises as outlined at the end of each chapter of the book and is to be used as a necessary tool in a framework to make the exercises meaningful.

Words are simply words on a page and will mean very little unless we integrate the processes and procedures and use them as guides to build a foundation for living a more peaceful happier life.

Now, we must seek to have a direct experience of discovering our own personal truths:

"Who am I?"

"What is working within my life and what is not?"

The chapter lessons are merely introductions to the ways in which we are able to leave the world of pain and shift to inner and outer peace. It is through our direct experiences we began our journey to reach the destiny life has set for all of us. May we all find the end toward which the practicing of our life experiences and our purpose was always geared.

Love and Light,

Christina and Dimitrios

Authors of *The Mind is the Map*

I

UNDERSTANDING OUR HABITUAL PATTERNS

How do We Create Our Reality?

MOST OF US would like a happier, healthier, more harmonious reality. In order to improve our reality, we must understand the mechanisms of its creation. Most of us feel that "things simply happen in our lives," or that we just feel "this way" or "that way." Few of us actually investigate how our reality is created.

> *We create our own reality by the way we interpret and react to the events in the ways we mentioned above. Our belief system creates our reality.*

Many of our problems are simply the result of our mistaken identity. We have learned to suppress what is naturally good within us. We have learned to mistrust others and compete against them, rather than cooperate and share with them. We have learned to be neurotic and fearful of new persons and situations. We have lost the ability to be open and loving, as we were when we were children.

We have been taught that we must fight for what we need, even at the others' expense. Such beliefs have been instilled in us as a way of "being smart" or "being successful." Many of us who have followed this philosophy find ourselves isolated, secluded and lonely.

We may have everything that society programmed our minds to believe was important, but do we have love, health, peace of mind, self-understanding, harmonious relationships or happiness?

Many of us set ourselves up for failure because of our habitual negative thinking and basic beliefs concerning our inadequacies. In the following pages, we will discuss the techniques by which we may recondition our thought processes and change our reality.

Our reality is constructed of two basic factors:

1. What is **happening** or has happened.

2. What we believe, and consequently how we feel about ourselves, in relation to what has happened, is happening or will happen.

It is our **belief system**, or programming, which creates our subjective perception of reality, while it is our past experiences that sets the writing on our walls. This writing is responsible for our conditioned habitual patterns.

Here is a story of how elephants are trained that will help
us understand the relationship between our past, our
beliefs, and our patterns that create our reality.

The Story

Self-Limiting Elephants

*Elephants born in captivity are restrained by a chain that attaches one leg to
a metal spike driven into the ground. This prevents them from roaming. They
become accustomed to the fact that, as long as the chain and spike are next
to them, they are unable to move. As they grow older, their minds become
programmed. When they see the spike and chain, they "believe" and accept
that they will not be able to move. They become so conditioned that when their
owners replace the spike and chain with a small rope and wooden peg next to
them, they make no efforts to step away from it because they "believe" they are
unable to do so. In truth, their actual power as adults is so great that they could
easily pull up a chain and spike of any size. Their programming, or "belief,"
however, allows this tiny rope and wooden peg to limit their movement.*

*We are all very much like these elephants. We allow the weaknesses, fears and
rejection we experienced as children to program us into a life in which we lack
power, peace, love and happiness. We become controlled by false childhood
assumptions we have made about our ability, strength and self-worth. We can
move away from these "pegs" of self-limitation, but we must choose to do so.*

EXPERIENCE

The Creation of Our Reality

The first factor in the creation of our reality is to identify with the experience itself. For example, we might find ourselves simply observing, or perhaps even fanaticizing or projecting our programming into the experience.

We need to look at the experience from four different perspectives.

1. **External perspective** includes events such as the following:

   We receive love, admiration, attention, gifts, money or success at some effort, or we are rejected, falsely accused, suffer a loss of someone or something important to us, or experience failure at some endeavor.

2. **Internal perspective**, such as thoughts about the past or future.

3. Our **emotions** or **thoughts** may become tangled and bundled with other emotions, such as when we feel anger or self-rejection when we observe that perhaps we have allowed ourselves to become aggressive or fearful.

4. **Body's Perspective** shows up as a subtler source of information. It might be the state of our hormones, chemical balance or energy level. We have all experienced days when we were more emotionally vulnerable, perhaps due to low life force energy.

TAKING OUR WOUNDS TO OUR HEART

Our heart is greater than our wounds.

The choice we all face constantly is whether we are taking our hurts to our head or to our heart. In our head, we can analyze them, find their causes and consequences, and coin words to speak and write about them. But no final healing is likely to come from that source.

We need to feel our emotions fully; let our wounds go down into our heart. Then we are able to allow ourselves to live them thoroughly and we will discover that they will not destroy us. "Our heart is greater than our wounds."

We have to let go of the mind's need to stay in control of our pain and trust in the healing power of our heart. Going to our heart with our wounds or any incomplete experiences we may have is not easy.

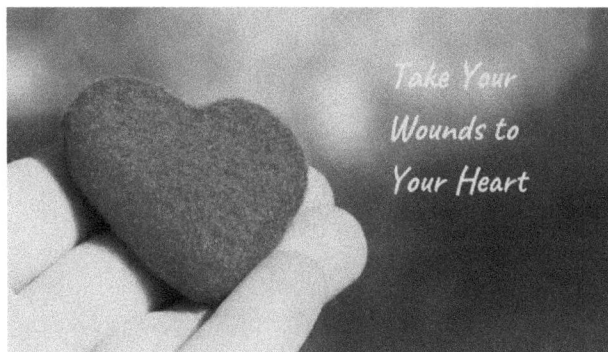

Take Your
Wounds to
Your Heart

Why was I wounded?

_____

_____

When?

_____

_____

How?

_____

By whom?

_____

_____

The answers to these questions will come from the mind, and although they may help us to understand ourselves better, at best, they only offer us a little distance from our pain.

Living a life of completeness and wholeness requires us to find the source of our emotions and transform our wounds so we can discover our true potential.

Caring for our soul requires that we become sensitive to any parts that are rough and begin to polish patterns that are rigid. Kindness is our loving Spirit in action, and if we are to be kind to the outside world, we must first be kind to our self and transform our fixed and inflexible ways.

DIALOGUE

Immersing Ourselves in The Great Experience called Life

Dimitrios Spanos:
Christina, it amazes me as to how we as a species
have collected incredible amounts of data, and studied and learned
so much about our Earth, planets, and the Universe. Although we have spent
hundreds of years understanding all kinds of natural phenomenon, we have not
been able to fully understand the workings of our own mind and eliminate our own
negative habitual patterns in order to bring total happiness and joy into our lives.

Christina Reeves:
Yes, Dimitrios, it is our destiny to fully
immerse ourselves in the great experience called life and to
live a self-approved life in harmony with the Universe, where we claim
our Divine birthright to create our best life. Some people don't want to revisit
their experiences and perhaps a deeper reason is that they really don't want others to
understand them completely, seemingly wanting to be invisible and to go through life
unknown to themselves or others. They may truly feel that this blindness provides them
safety and freedom. However, life is meant to be lived and experienced fully. With this
mindset, they are only able to live a very small part of the reality of who they are and why
they are here. When they live a very small and limited part of who they really are, they
become unsatisfied with the life they are imagining and creating for themselves and
may say things like, "What happened to my life?" or "Is this all there is?"

THE EVALUATION OF OUR EXPERIENCES

As these experiences pass into the mind, the mind evaluates them, seeking to determine whether they are supportive of or endangering to our basic needs..

1. If our subconscious programming determines them to be supportive, we feel relaxed, happy and loving.

2. If we conclude that they are endangering, we experience fear as well as a wide variety of other emotions, such as pain, disillusionment, bitterness, injustice, depression, jealousy, envy, anger and hate.

Our emotional state constitutes the greater portion of our subjective personal reality. It is not so much what happens in our life that creates our reality, but rather how we perceive and react to what happens (or to what we imagine is happening or will happen).

We create our own reality by the way we interpret and react to the events in the ways we mentioned above. Our belief system creates our reality.

OUR PROGRAMMING

If we want to be happy, we need to transcend our automatic response of habitual, mechanical emotional reactions. We need to understand why we automatically react in certain ways, such as with fear or anger, and how we can begin to free ourselves from undesirable emotional responses. Otherwise we are not free. We are under the control of the programming of our childhood, our past, our lack of clarity and our lack of awareness. We are "asleep" to our real personal nature and the true nature of the reality surrounding us.

RECOGNIZING OUR PATTERNS

What patterns do I see?

MAKING IT PERSONAL

Our patterns are part of our human experience. When a pattern is triggered by an experience, we feel it by way of our emotions, and we habitually react to it and allow it to influence decisions that have important consequences for all our lives. Understanding our emotions and patterns can be considered a form of art requiring discovery, awareness, and creativity.

The starting point is not struggling with the pattern. Instead, fully accept what is occurring and remain open to sensing the freedom of change. This is easier said than done. It takes a lot of practice to remain open to intense emotions without our habitual responses of defending our territory.

Staying open, we can relax in the midst of emotional upheaval and appreciate it for what it is. How we experience this openness depends on both the situation and our perceptions of it. By accepting that we have been triggered and opening up to the situation, we can pay attention to our feelings and our surroundings; sensing what is needed with an open mind and heart. This will help us to discriminate between reacting from our habitual patterns and move us toward more useful and mindful responses.

Acknowledging that sometimes our past responses did not work very well for us, we start from the present moment and look for its creative potential. We reconsider the situation and we look at the details from various perspectives and with fresh eyes—remaining sensitive to our feelings.

EMOTIONAL HIJACKING

Did You Know?

Emotional hijacking is a very unpleasant feeling, as it is a state of mind where we feel that we are no longer in charge of our own thoughts and emotions. During these times, we might feel that someone has misunderstood us and treated us unfairly; thus we may feel that our choices are limited. In such cases, we might lose self-control, or we might feel overwhelmed by our emotions. At this point, the mind has become emotionally hijacked..

FIGHT OR FLIGHT

Hijacking of the mind feels like an outside attack, where the perpetrator seems to take illegal control of something of ours and we feel the need to defend it. What is really happening is that our rational mind is overloaded by our emotions and interferes with our reasoning. What is remarkable is that during the hijacking process, our mind is taken over in less than six seconds, which is almost the same rate as a full inhale and exhale.

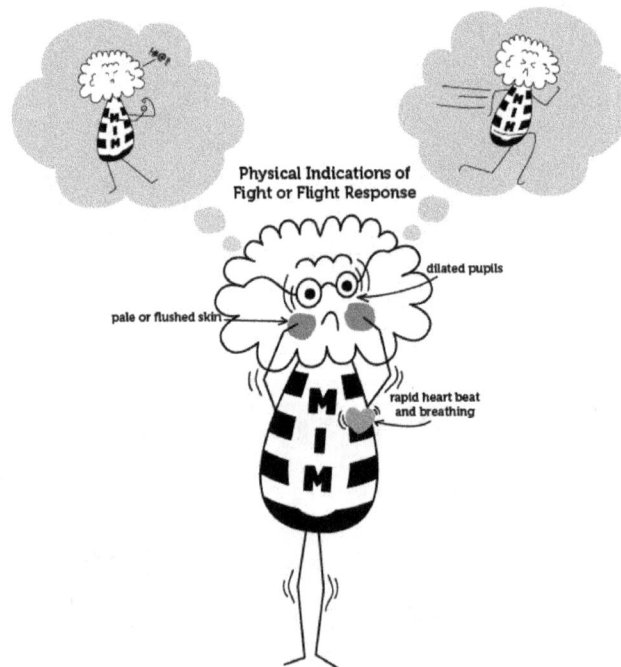

Physical Indications of Fight or Flight Response

dilated pupils

pale or flushed skin

rapid heart beat and breathing

EXERCISE

The questions below are not always easy to answer, and many beginners at this process of self-discovery feel frustrated. Our suggestion is to try turning this frustration into genuine curiosity about getting to know yourself on a deeper level. Remain curious and play with the mystery and wonder of all that is.

Ask yourself the following discovery question:

How often do I react to people and situations based on old habits (perceiving, thinking, feeling and behaving)?

After you've taken time to think about it, ask yourself:

have you ever noticed that you become defensive?

Before even realizing it, you automatically respond as if those old experiences were happening again (defense mechanisms). All of us have developed habitual patterns of behavior, and all automatic reactions are based on past experiences.

What is it that is actually, bothering me?

_____

_____

_____

_____

What patterns do I see?

_____

_____

_____

_____

What do I feel about these patterns?

_____

_____

_____

_____

What triggers me?

_____

_____

_____

_____

What habitual behavior patterns do I engage in when I have been triggered?

_____

_____

_____

_____

What do I believe about myself or about others (consciously or subconsciously) which is forcing me to behave in this manner?

_____

_____

_____

_____

REFLECTION

Our behaviors are the result of these complicated belief structures. Reality is different for each one of us, but how we perceive reality is how we create reality. The question is that of consciousness. The more conscious we are, the closer we get to reality. In order to do so, we need to keep examining our patterns, beliefs and assumptions, and we need to transform them to ones that serve us better—ones that can lead us towards living happier more peaceful lives.

During self-discovery, you may notice a number of external events that influence your beliefs, thoughts and emotions, but not always for the better. In addition, certain decisions may have kept you from seeing greater opportunities for growth.

Past Limited Beliefs:

Where am I making limited decisions?

_____

_____

_____

What do I believe about the experience that keeps limiting me?

_____

_____

_____

Am I acting on old childhood conclusions or childhood survival skills that are no longer helpful?

_____

_____

_____

What is it from my past that keeps influencing my present?

_____

_____

_____

How do my past experiences keep creating my automatic modes of reactions and behavior?

_____

_____

_____

Why do I believe about myself, others or life itself?

_____

_____

_____

Did I intentionally choose those beliefs or was I just following opinions and ideas of others?

_____

_____

_____

What beliefs do I need to transform to achieve my dreams and bring the utmost happiness in my life?

_____

_____

_____

How might I overcome the pre-conceived experiences of my mind's programming and take full responsibility for my own thoughts and feelings?

_____

_____

_____

Triggers:

What would it take to stop blaming the outside world and to stop overreacting to different issues?

_____

_____

_____

What are the triggers that keep causing major hardship in my life?

_____

_____

_____

What kind of activity am I involved in when the trigger takes place?

_____

_____

_____

What outside events (if any) are connected with these triggers?

_____

_____

_____

In what ways can I be flexible enough to create more possibilities and choices in my behaviors?

_____

_____

_____

HAVE FUN JOURNALING

Through journaling, we begin to practice the art of discovery. We learn to recognize our habitual patterns, discover how they affect us and those around us, and learn to work with them.

Do not try to solve all the pattern problems in this exercise. Instead, simply allow yourself time to process them and allow more questions to come up.

Our patterns, thoughts, and beliefs have caused us many problems and suffering in our relationships, our families, our wealth, our society, and with ourselves.

Learning to identify and work with these habitual patterns is the key to transforming our lives.

Our patterns are running all the time and cause destruction everywhere.

Begin a journal about your experience with patterns. Write about how your life might be driven by undesirable habitual patterns.

Be sure to include the following:

Where did they come from?

_____

_____

_____

Do a reality test on what you believe. It is true for you?

_____

_____

_____

What happens when you get highjacked by these patterns?

See how you react, attack, and become defensive.

Note any fight and/or flight patterns you might have.

_____

_____

_____

What are the top five patterns you see in your life?

_____

_____

_____

What patterns would you like to change?

_____

_____

_____

THE PROCESS OF TRANSFORMATION

Here are three steps to assist the process of transformation:

- **Discovery.** Notice what you are doing. Pay attention to how you respond habitually to any event in your life.

- **Realization.** Do something different. Consider responding to the experience in a very different way. This will loosen up the pattern.

- **Breakthrough.** Make it a way of life. Keep doing something different. This will bring about your own wisdom, strength, and fundamental goodness of the heart and mind.

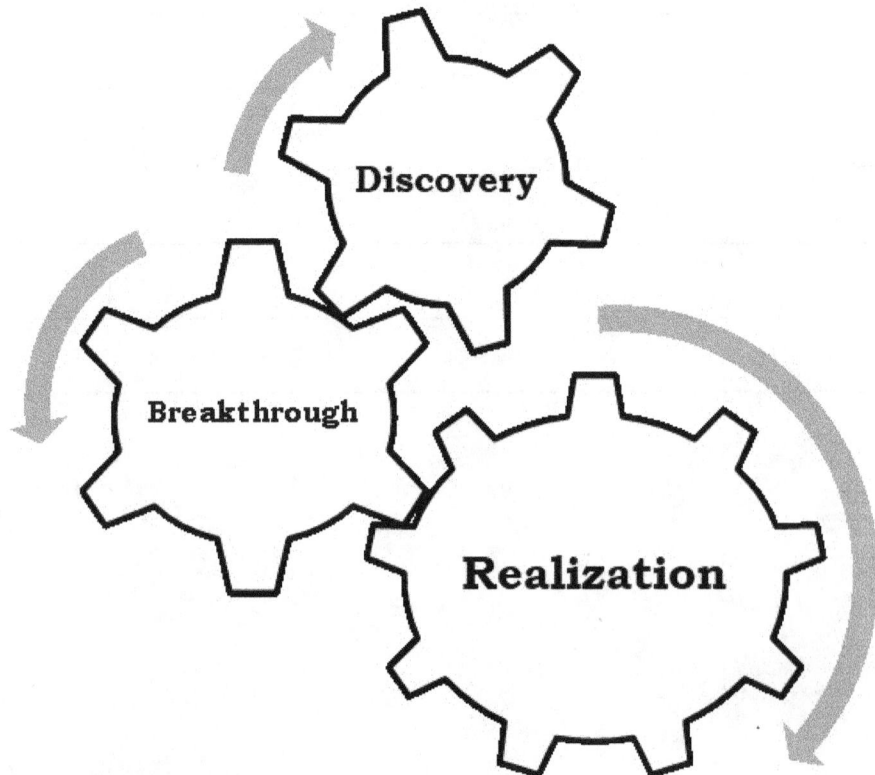

CONNECT WITH OTHERS

Start a conversation with a friend or loved one sharing your experiences and insights from your journaling.

Practice active listening while encouraging the other person to tell their story of where they are on the discovery of their patterns.

Reflect with your friend or partner on both stories and discuss any missed opportunities to recognize a pattern or to choose a better response when triggered.

Discuss how any needs, attachments or beliefs might keep us stuck in our patterns interfering with a more favorable outcome.

What might you have said or done to make a different choice rather than act out your habitual patterned response?

To assist you, we have included a possible needs list and some common behavior patterns in the appendices in the back of this book.

Milestones

Few of us have a very intimate knowledge of our patterns. By accepting our undesirable habitual patterns, we can learn to gently and skillfully work with them, soften our sharp edges, and gain confidence in our ability to respond to our experiences with wisdom.

A simple shift in attitude can help us recognize and uncover the hidden potential and/or gift for every circumstance we find ourselves in. Allowing the inner light to flow into the outer world brings to us a new understanding and fulfillment in every experience, including every perceived setback.

Our negative habitual patterns turn from compost to fertile ground where we can plant new seeds of Awareness. Each time you discover a pattern accurately, you have reached another milestone.

Celebrate these milestones by recognizing them and slow down to take a moment to feel what is true for you instead of simply answering with an automatic habitual response.

Creating our dreams embodies all of our longings and desires. They hold the promise of love through our spiritual connect as possibilities to be fulfilled. It is important to realize that we are co-creators with our source of all that is, therefore there is nothing we cannot create in our life. If we are love, then it is love that we will call to us. In fact, our spiritual evolution intensifies each time we claim our good through calling to us that which we want and desire. By allowing our dreams the time and space to unfold we gain clarity about what we want and give them the opportunity to manifest. Claiming them is how our dreams come true.

Meditation

Close your eyes sit quietly and take in several deep cleansing breaths. Scan your body for any tension and release the tension by breathing into the area. Relax your shoulders and jaw and allow your eyes and behind your eyes to relax. Adjust your body so your neck and back are in alignment with yourself. Feel this relaxation flow through you as you continue to breathe evenly and easily. Feel yourself as you relax deeper now and ease down into your body and into the stillness.

If you are feeling sensitive and vulnerable, you can move now into a place of awareness. Support yourself by relaxing into awareness in all of your external experiences and realize that life has the ability to run itself. Activate your awareness, simply imagining the experience you wish to address in this meditation as if it were on a wide, blank screen in front of you. Now imagine stepping back from the experience and becoming the watcher. From this vantage point, notice yourself in the experience. What are you doing, thinking and feeling?

Now look at the actual experience itself; is what's happening clear? Are you reacting to something that was triggered within you? Remember, nothing can cause you to feel anything other than what is in your own mind. Your thoughts create your feelings. Notice the cause and effect of the experience. Now observe the processing of the experience and ask yourself if what you have done or said is in alignment with who you would like to be. Now ask yourself how the other might be feeling; what might be triggering the other in this experience?

Now tune back into your body and check your energy field. Feeling the areas of tension can give you a sense of what is blocked within you, and by affirming yourself and learning to use your mind, you are able to release what is bothering you. Open your mind to receive your highest guidance and listen carefully for direct knowledge that will support your well-being. Ask to see where you need to forgive yourself or another, and ask this to be brought into your consciousness. Ask yourself, "What would love do right now?" Using the mind in this way gives you mastery over your physical body energetically and helps you create an energy field which is whole, clear and purified.

While in awareness as the observer, if you noticed even one hint of clarity to any of these questions, you have in your hands a thread that could lead beyond thought, feeling or reaction. While there are many perspectives to view the experience, there is only one reality, and every clue must lead eventually to the same place where the laws of creation operate freely, which is awareness itself. Each of us creates our own reality; we need only observe to know the truth of this statement.

II

❧

OUR LIFE FORCE ENERGY

Life is a Dance with the Universe

"Life has no other discipline to impose, if we would but realize it, than to accept life unquestioningly. Everything we shut our eyes to, everything we run away from, everything we deny, denigrate, or despise, serves to defeat us in the end. What seems nasty, painful, evil, can become a source of beauty, joy, and strength, if faced with an open mind. Every moment is a golden one for those who have the vision to recognize it as such." -Henry Miller

WHAT IS LIFE FORCE ENERGY?

Life Force Energy is exactly what it sounds like. It is the Universal Energy that **gives life to all things**. Our thoughts are energy and give rise to our emotions, which in turn are simply energy in motion like invisible clouds hovering above and around our physical body. **High-frequency emotions**, such as **love and joy**, are **bright**, while **lower frequency** emotions are **dimmer** and sometimes **dark**.

Nature's intelligence functions with effortless ease, harmony and love. We can learn to harness this Life Force Energy to create success and good fortune with the same effortless ease using our conscious awareness. **Everything in our Universe is made of energy**, and the universal laws of physics tell us that like energy attracts like energy. We must become an energetic vibrational match to what it is that we wish to attract into our experiences.

Following the laws of nature, the law of least effort as nature teaches us, we will learn to **accept people, situations, circumstances and events as they occur** and this raises our Life Force Energy. Within the flow of Universal energy lays the wisdom of uncertainty… in the wisdom of uncertainty lays the freedom from our past, from the known, which is the prison of past conditioning. In our willingness to step into the unknown is the field of all possibilities; a place where we can surrender ourselves to the creative mind that orchestrates the dance of the universe.

In order to help ourselves and understand others, first, we must understand the nature of our being. **Humans are energy beings**, in fact, every part of us is made of energy particles: including every organ, cell, membrane, bone, fiber, tissue and muscle in our physical body. In addition, all of our thoughts, emotions and spirit are also made of energy particles. **We are an intricate and complicated combination of pure energy.**

VIBRATIONS AND FREQUENCIES

Life Force Energy enters our body through our breath and flows through the acupuncture meridians and vitalizes the organs and tissues. When the flow of this Life Force Energy is depleted or not in balance, this will ultimately lead to disease in the physical body. These depletions and imbalances come about as a result of physical and psychological factors. Through our mental powers, we have the ability to increase and rebalance the flow of Life Force Energy throughout the body and, thus, combat disease.

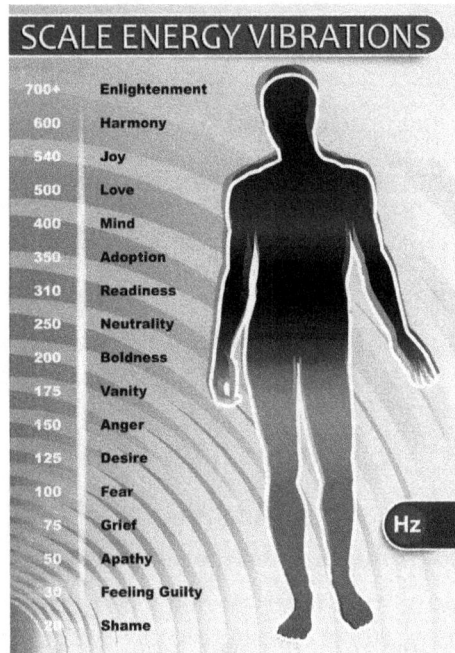

SCALE ENERGY VIBRATIONS

Hz	
700+	Enlightenment
600	Harmony
540	Joy
500	Love
400	Mind
350	Adoption
310	Readiness
250	Neutrality
200	Boldness
175	Vanity
150	Anger
125	Desire
100	Fear
75	Grief
50	Apathy
	Feeling Guilty
	Shame

Each level of energy vibration holds your own particular resonance made of physical energy. The problem is that some people are creating with conscious awareness of this process, while others continue to live life unconsciously. To live a conscious life is to become aware of our own thoughts, actions and deeds.

It is easy to raise our Life Force Energy when **we view ourselves as consciousness** rather than as separate bodies and minds. If we want to experience the joyful divinity of every present moment, we will need to let go of any beliefs that limit and distort it.

Our Thoughts and Feelings as Energies

Feelings of Happiness:

When we are lost in our emotions, we are unable to experience higher levels of energy. This occurs by setting particular conditions on our life experiences which if they are not fulfilled, we are refusing to feel happiness. Many of our emotions can distance us from our happiness and we will never find the answer to our experiences solely with logic.

The simple law of physics that states "like energy always attracts like energy," so if this is true then we know that our negative thoughts are resonating to a particular frequency that will absolutely draw to our life more of the same negative experiences. Hence we have heard the saying, "be careful what you think" … thinking is a form of energy in motion.

Feelings of Separateness:

The biggest obstacle to that experience is the illusory feeling of separateness created by our senses when in fact we are one spirit, one with all energy, and even one with all matter. This feeling of being separate from others and the forces around us causes us to fear and develop defense mechanisms that lower our Life Force Energy and seriously obstruct our happiness.

You might be saying to yourself about now, "OK, if thought is a creation and if I change my thinking why don't I see the effect of that change working in my life?" This is a great question!

Thoughts as Energies:

Thoughts and mind are not the same. Thoughts are things, and thoughts are action. The moment you have a thought you have created an action. Just like the spoken word is a thing, the moment you speak you have created an action. Thoughts and words are creative actions just as a deed is an action. All are creative actions that create the energy of your being. They are all energies at a level of creation.

It is not enough to simply want, to intend or to use your will power to change your thoughts. The basis for these thoughts is your belief system. The first supporting thought you ever had on the issue will always be based on an early belief system.

Feeling our Emotions:

One example of this might be an unconscious decision to resist feeling things fully. As a child perhaps, what was happening around you in your environment was simply too overwhelming for you. Operating on this level means you may have developed a pattern of resistance to fully feeling your emotions. By not fully feeling our emotions, we continue to create the same experiences over and over again; thus recreating the same outcomes.

Operating on another level, we often tend to look for ourselves where we are not, meaning we look outside of ourselves to others for self-worth and validation of who we are. This causes a feeling of being separate or isolated from others.

WE ATTRACT WHAT WE ARE

Did You Know?

When living in an emotionally higher vibrational state most of the time, our interactions with others dramatically improve. We are much happier, and we attract to us more options and opportunities to live our best life.

Reality Check

In other scenarios, we may find ourselves trying to force outcomes using manipulative behaviors to get our needs or expectations met because of our attachment to things or to people outside of ourselves. And of course, when our expectations or needs do not get met, we blame others or life itself for our reality. We may have even created a reality whereby we have a tendency to overreact when things don't turn out the way we wanted them to.

When we live our life by **choice**, we are living consciously in our present moment. When we live our life by **chance**, we are creating our life through a series of unconscious beliefs and habitual reactionary behaviors.

One of my favorite stories is the story of Lambert the Sheepish Lion. It became a famous Disney cartoon some years ago.

The Story

Lambert the Sheepish Lion

> Lambert was a lion cub that had lived with a flock of sheep from the time he was born. Because of that, he thought he was a sheep. One spring night, Lambert and the flock were sleeping peacefully. Suddenly Lambert heard the scary howl of a wolf in the distance. Because Lambert thought he was a sheep, he began to tremble.
>
> The howl grew louder, and the wolf came closer and began dragging one of the sheep away. Suddenly Lambert felt a strong feeling inside that he had never felt before. Like lightning, he ran toward the wolf to save the sheep.
>
> Just then Lambert realized something. "I am not a sheep. I am not the son of a sheep. I am the son of a lion!" Lambert thought. When he chased off the wolf and protected the sheep, he knew his true nature.

We are like the sheepish lion. The sheep represent our human nature—our personality—which moans, fears, complains and worries. The lion is the spiritual aspect of our being, which is a source of great power, wisdom, creativity, goodness and love.

"All there is, is Consciousness." It is here that we will know the experience of dissolution and bliss that comes when the mind has been liberated and the heart has been illuminated from within.

EXPERIENCE

Keeping our Energy High and Harmonious

The quantity and quality of our energy flow deeply affects our emotions, thoughts and reactions. The quality of our relationships, productivity, creativity and health all depend upon creating a high level of harmoniously flowing energy. Our inner harmony is deeply affected by our relationships with those around us. The opposite is even truer: **our relationships with others will simply mirror our relationships with ourselves**.

Our Reactions

We react to situations and events in various external and internal ways. We may withdraw from the experience or become aggressive, pushing others away. We may live in denial of what we feel and what is happening. We may attempt to communicate about the problem, or avoid communicating at all. We might become sarcastic or perhaps plead for help. We might nag or complain continuously. We might act unconcerned or aloof even when we are boiling inside. We may make various inner efforts to overcome our feelings, or we might simply suppress them.

It is important to remember that **our reactions then become triggers for others' emotional mechanisms**, and subsequently, their reactions towards us. Then their reactions become new stimuli which trigger our emotional reactions, and we become like two or more programmed robots interacting in totally unconscious, mechanical and often disagreeable ways. Our reactions are limited to the ways we have been programmed as children to react in relation to each experience.

Our reactions also become triggers for our own emotional mechanisms. As we observe ourselves reacting, we often judge ourselves and feel disappointment, shame or self-rejection or even fear that we might lose control or be totally rejected by others. In such a case, our reactions become triggers for a secondary emotional mechanism. For example, if we observe that we are reacting aggressively, or the opposite, that we are not reacting at all, we might reject ourselves, thus adding new emotions to the original ones which created our original reactions. Such secondary mechanisms are quite frequent at each stage of this process. **We have emotions about the emotions we have. We have beliefs and emotions about the beliefs which we observe. We have beliefs and emotions concerning our reactions.**

Discharging our energy onto others causes us to lose energy!

Our emotions are often expressed as uncontrolled words or actions. In some cases, we simply throw our emotional energy onto others by accusing, intimidating, blaming and generally bombarding them with this negatively charged energy. The negative energy which we discharge to others causes them to develop negative feelings towards us, and causes a great burden and can even destroy our relationships. Why do we allow this to happen? It is because we have not learned to understand and deal effectively with our emotional nature. We are not interested in suppressing our emotions here, but rather in observing, analyzing, understanding, accepting and transforming them, usually in this order.

DIALOGUE

The Flow of Life Force Energy

Dimitrios Spanos:

Christina, our Life Force Energy is our infrastructure. Nature's elements and the Universe provide our life-giving energy, animates our body, and channels it through our mind and soul. All forces of nature, sunlight, air, and wind are manifestations of the Life Force energy and we, in turn, are a true reflection of their natural beauty. We all experience the beauty and sustenance of nature. We get to see the sunshine each day; the reflection of light on Earth; the elegance of mountains; trees; the liveliness of the crystals; minerals; the blooming of flowers, and the ocean's rhythmic movement.

Our sun's light transforms our own light while our etheric body takes the sun's rays and creates energy and vitality for our physical cells. Our lungs take oxygen from the air and transport it through 60,000 miles of vessels to deliver it everywhere in our body in order to keep us alive. The spectacular and wondrous ebb and flow of the Life Force Energy creates a blissful harmony within our body circulating in our blood and influencing our breathing patterns.

Christina Reeves:

Thank you, Dimitrios. This lovely word picture truly depicts the flow of our Life Force Energy. Energy is never about something or someone out there—it is always an inside job. Now that we understand that everything in our world is created of energy and how this energy creates energetic footprints and fields of energy around each one of us, it is important to protect our own energetic field. One of the most difficult challenges in life is learning not to take things personally. We must try not to take on the energy of others in an experience as our own. Sometimes there are numerous others involved in our experiences, all with opinions of their own, and often these conflicts can cause even more misunderstandings. This only exasperates the issues with so many opinions creating even more conflicting energy and issues in the larger scope of things. Unfortunately, we cannot fix others. We can only learn to remain in our moment-to-moment interactions, holding a loving space for them as we ourselves continue on the path of self-realization.

RECOGNIZING OUR PATTERNS

Understanding Our Emotions

MAKING IT PERSONAL

When caught in a lower vibrational frequency, things can seem hard to overcome. Choosing in a determined fashion to observe ourselves and how we react in stressful situations, objectively looking at why we felt and reacted in a particular way, and seeking ways to dissolve any negative emotional hooks to past events empowers us to greatly improve our life experiences and live a much happier life.

No matter how overwhelmed, stressed, angry or anxious we might feel during challenging moments, we have within us an innate power to change the way we approach these challenges by simply shifting our thoughts.

Some of our emotional releases can be very painful. Because of that, we often tend to repress them deep within, not wanting to feel them again. No matter how intense and painful a release might be, we feel much better afterwards. The more we clear ourselves from accumulated lower frequency emotions, the higher our frequency will rise and the happier we'll become.

Ignoring your Life Force Energy can be dangerous. It can cause us to become ill, stay in a relationship too long, or keep us stuck in a business or job that doesn't quite feel right. Whenever you feel torn or confused about how to increase your Life Force Energy with a particular situation, ask yourself: "What am I pretending not to know?" Once you get your answer, be bold enough to listen to it and take action.

Then comes the next step: "What am I grateful for?"

Maintaining a state of gratitude sends out a vibrational signal to the Universe to bring more of that into our lives. Gratitude is a higher form of Life Force Energy. Lower vibrational frequencies such as fear, scarcity, and doubt simply cannot live in a grateful heart. So, if you're experiencing the lower energy vibration of pain or discomfort, the easiest way to shift out of it is to ask yourself what you're grateful for. This will help you relax and increase your Life Force Energy.

REFLECTION

How can I hold the space for increasing my Life Force Energy?

It helps to remember that we create our own reality. No matter what "negative" things you are currently experiencing, something about your way of being had initially welcomed them in. Remember our physics lessons, "like energy attracts like energy;" and our energetic footprint will attract to us like a magnet what we already are. We don't get what we want; we get what we are. If you don't like the reality you're living in, you must be brave enough to change something internally.

After getting clear about how YOU are the space for what is occurring in your life, if you want to find an evolved solution to almost any problem, sit on this question and see what solutions come up.

"What would love do right now?"

ASK YOURSELF:

What are my blind spots or areas of improvement?

_____

_____

_____

List areas in your current life or style of living where you might be losing or leaking your Life Force Energy.

_____

_____

_____

How do you think that you might be standing in your own way?

_____

_____

_____

List some things you might want to change that are draining your Life Force Energy.

_____

_____

_____

HAVE FUN JOURNALING

Begin a journal about your Life Force Energy's experience. Be sure to answer the questions above in great detail. Next, write about an experience you had or are having—one where you could feel your Life Force Energy at a low point. Include the emotions you felt at that time. As you write, feel the difference in your energy field.

Next, write about an experience you had—one where you could feel your Life Force Energy at a very high point. Again, record any emotions you were feeling and once again feel the difference in your energy field.

To assist you in this exercise, we have included a list of possible emotions in the appendices of this book.

If you want to live a powerful life, you have to ask powerful questions. Here are just a few questions to consider:

What is the highest and best use of my energy?

_____

_____

_____

_____

_____

In today's busy world, time seems to be the one commodity we all are yearning for. But in order to feel like we're making the most of our Life Force Energy, we must first know what matters most to us. When you get clear and prioritize what's most important to you, you won't feel so trapped by lower level energies.

How do I define my own energetic vibrational footprint?

_____

_____

_____

_____

So many people today are chasing success and sacrificing their time, their relationships and their sanity to get "there" at any cost, without even considering the cost of their Life Force Energy.

Stop to think about how you define your level of Life Force Energy.

_____

_____

_____

_____

Before you set out on your next big journey toward success, be sure to define what it looks like to you first. Then feel into your vision of your success. Using your imagination, try on different scenarios and see what each one feels like from an energetic point of view.

Will my choices give me energy or deplete my energy?

_____

_____

_____

_____

_____

When journaling, be prepared not to have all the questions or answers. Remain open. Our tendency is to try to solve all the problems rather than allowing ourselves to have time to process and allow more questions to come up. Although it may seem inefficient, even when we feel sure that we have the answer in our mind, it is often best to complete the journal entry with a question rather than an answer. This question will then work in the subconscious mind, calling forth answers, intuition (tuition from within), inspiration and guidance from within.

CONNECT WITH OTHERS

Who's on your team? Take some time to identify some of the key players who can help you on your journey. Who do you know who can provide you with motivation? Expertise? Distraction? A listening ear? On the flip side, who's getting in your way of achieving your goals? Be mindful of negative people who might be draining your Life Force Energy.

Start a conversation with a friend or loved one sharing your experience and your insights from your journaling. Practice active listening while encouraging the other person to tell their stories related to their Life Force Energy.

Reflect with your friend or partner on both stories and discuss any missed opportunities to make choices that raise our energy field and see how any needs, attachments or beliefs might have interfered.

We'll never truly be able to see ourselves objectively; therefore, we need to look outside of ourselves to get honest feedback about how we're showing up in life. Turn to those around you for an unbiased review.

You can ask them:

- What are my blind spots or areas of improvement?

- In what areas am I getting in my own way?

The key is to ask with a genuine curiosity to want to learn more about how others see you so that you can improve yourself.

To assist you in determining any needs you might have, we have included a list of possible needs in the appendices in the back of this book.

Milestones

Many people believe they are merely helpless victims of their circumstances. But in actuality, our external circumstances are the direct result of our Life Force being directed by either our conscious or subconscious intent to create our exact life circumstances.

Few of us have a very intimate contact with our Life Force Energy. When someone asks what we are feeling, we often answer vaguely, "bad, unhappy, upset, disturbed and negative." We want to get more specific when describing our emotional state and we also want to feel into our energy level.

Each time you take a moment to feel into your energy and name the emotions accurately that either heightened or lowered your energy level, you have reached another milestone.

Celebrate these milestones by recognizing them and slow down to take a moment to feel what is true for you instead of simply answering with an automatic habitual response. Try feeling things fully on all levels: emotional, physical and energetic.

To assist you with this, we have included a list of possible emotions in the appendices in the back of this book.

Meditation

This is a morning meditation; allow yourself to wake up happy each morning, fresh and renewed, fill yourself with life force energy to begin your day. I recommend waking early enough to experience the peace that the morning can bring. This could mean waking before you begin your day by initiating a routine of mindful awareness listening to your heart.

Feel the silence of a quiet house and before you open your eyes and before your feet hit the floor, ask your "I Am" presence to join fully with you now. Do this meditation before any thought enters your mind about how you will spend your day. Be aware of the essence of awakening from the dreaming state. Notice how wonderful it feels to wake up in this peaceful calm space.

The key to doing this meditation correctly is to let go of the mind stuff. The endless sound of our critical voice is likened to a tape recorder that plays in our heads, and effectively keeps us from feeling our inner peace.

We are creatures of habit in how we wake up in the morning and with how handle the routine of everyday life. Notice how waking up in this manner and as you ease deeper into the calm peaceful state that there is a strong desire to stay in the flow of life. Many have experienced new and inspired thoughts arising from this deeper inner place. Once you have experienced this miracle, it is hard to forget that feeling. It is a mysterious experience that seems to call you to your greater destiny. It is a moment that suddenly fills you with a new vision and perhaps even your life purpose.

Now think of any questions or problems that need answering. Use prayer to affirm that the answers will come to you easily, and remember to pray from the place of absolute knowing that your prayer will be answered.

Now close your eyes and try to visualize any possible outcomes in the form of image/images and be mindful of any feelings that come over you. Now move your attention from the problem and become the watcher or observer and notice how easily it is to calm our minds enough to keep ourselves watchful for these exciting opportunities to understand yourself better. Stay in a state of gratitude for a minute or two and set your attention to remaining alert to any messages, visions or insight you may receive; accept and trust these Divine messages.

III

AWARENESS IS THE COMPASS

WHAT IS AWARENESS?

Awareness

is just itself—

pure, alive, alert, silent and full of

potential.

It is a feeling of being **at ease** with **everything** and everyone around us. It is a peace of mind and a **sense of well-being**, as well as an **inner knowing** that all is well, despite the circumstances we are in at the **present moment**.

ACHIEVING AWARENESS

When we are in **Awareness**, we become the **observer** of the mind, body, and the current experience we happen to be in, and we can observe the subtle conversations between our mind and the body. This is one of the practices of **Emotional Intelligence**. By using Emotional Intelligence in this way, we can have a profound impact that contributes to our wellbeing.

First, we must learn to experience our self, **free of the mind stuff**, **our stories** and **self-images**. To experience our true self, we have to move away from the stories we have told ourselves about our self-image and any thoughts about ourselves in the experiences we are having right here and now in the present moment. We must be completely absent of thoughts and self-images, which obscure who we really are. As long as we continue to respond and react to our experiences with **long-ingrained emotional patterns and mechanisms**, we will continue to feel the same emotions, do what we have always done and attract the same behaviors and events.

It helps to remember that **"People do what they do and it's that simple."** They too have been programmed with a set of beliefs which cause them to behave in habitual patterns. By accepting things and others as they are, we can learn to take **responsibility** for all of our experiences, and even for all those we see as problems.

A simple change in attitude and a shift to awareness can help us evaluate our potential for fulfilment in every perceived positive experience and every perceived setback.

Step into Awareness. Step BACK and observe!

Visualize the experience as if it is playing itself out on a **movie screen** in front of you and realize this experience is just an **illusion**; a story that you are playing a part in and so are the others.

THE THREE PARTS OF AWARENESS

Consider Awareness as a place within us that allows us to see all aspects of our experiences, taking in all the varying perspectives, enabling us to create a more loving and conscious response to life.

When we are in Awareness, we become the observer of the mind, body and current experience we happen to be in, and we can observe the subtle conversations between our mind and the body. This is one of the practices of Emotional Intelligence and using Emotional Intelligence in this way, we can have a profound impact that contributes to our wellbeing.

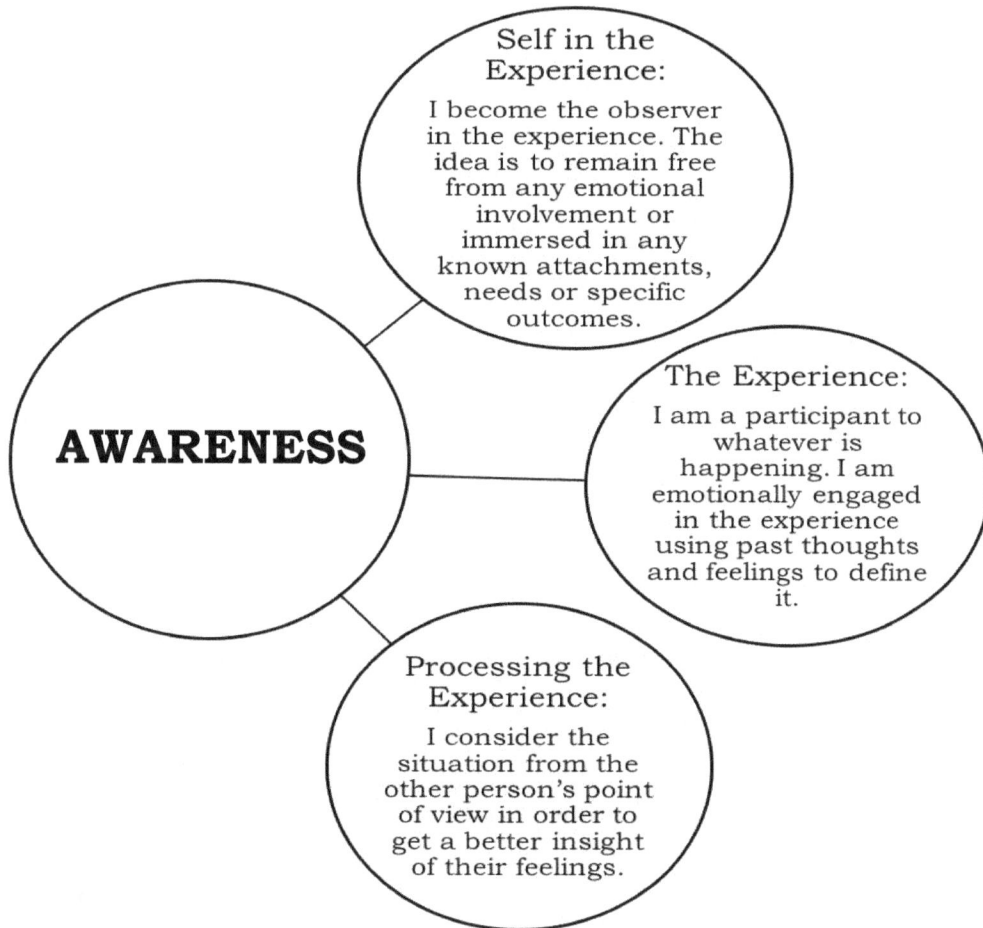

Self in the Experience:

I become the observer in the experience. The idea is to remain free from any emotional involvement or immersed in any known attachments, needs or specific outcomes.

AWARENESS

The Experience:

I am a participant to whatever is happening. I am emotionally engaged in the experience using past thoughts and feelings to define it.

Processing the Experience:

I consider the situation from the other person's point of view in order to get a better insight of their feelings.

The Story

Overcoming an Obstacle

In an ancient city many years ago, the Ruler of this city placed a large stone on a roadway to obstruct the way. He wanted to see if anyone in his Kingdom would respond to the obstruction, and so he positioned himself to watch the road where others could not see him. He witnessed that many people, including a lot of prominent people in his Kingdom travelling the road, simply walked around the boulder.

These same people protested in anger and blamed the Ruler for not clearing the roads, but not a single one of them took any initiative to solve the problem themselves (and for other travelers) by trying to remove the stone.

After some time, a peasant returning from the market place walked down the road with his arms filled with vegetables and other goods. When he saw the obstruction in the road, he laid down his packages, and after much struggling, he was able to push the boulder out of the way for others to pass.

After the peasant gathered his packages and started back on his way, he noticed a small bag tied with a string. It had seemingly appeared out of nowhere, lying on the road where he had removed the stone. Curious to see what it could be, he opened the small sack and within it were many gold coins along with a letter from the Ruler thanking him for removing the boulder from the roadway.

Every obstacle we come across in life is a gift providing us with opportunities to see and learn from our circumstances. While some ignore the gifts, some others see opportunities through their kind hearts and generosity to service and making a difference. They have a willingness to find solutions in life and simply get things done.

EXPERIENCE

Think about any experience you are having in the present moment and take a moment to step back from the experience. Take several deep breaths and step into Awareness. Step back and observe. By saying this, I do not mean for you to activate a fight or flight response. Simply visualize the experience as if it is playing itself out on a movie screen in front of you and realize this experience is just an illusion, a story that you are playing a part in and so are the others.

CALMING THE DISTURBANCES: Using Awareness, we can constantly calm our mind to clearly see each experience as it is. An observation of how our mind functions exposes the simple fact that the mind is not very organized; we often quickly shift from one subject to another. Our minds are at the mercy of a web of thoughts, beliefs and assumptions that pull us here and there, into both the past and future.

BECOME AWARE OF MOTIVES: Seeing our experiences from a place of awareness, we become constantly aware of our actions and motives, and those of the others within the experience. When we are fully aligned with our highest self, we are operating from a place of awareness. When we step into awareness and observe the experience, the mind is no longer searching our data bank for answers.

Did You Know?

THE POWER OF AWARENESS

Awareness helps us cleanse the lens of our perception of ourselves and others, allowing us to see the old beliefs and programming that no longer serve us.

DIALOGUE

Our Responsibility is our Response-Ability

Dimitrios Spanos

Yes Christina, response-ability is what stops us from charging ahead and living a fuller life. Over the course of our life, we develop a web of beliefs, thoughts and emotions. We create images of our personality and the personalities of others until one day we realize that these images are not part of our truth, but simply our perceptions, assumptions and external reflections.

Christina Reeves:

Our responsibility is our response-ability. Taking responsibility means not blaming anyone or anything for our situation, our feelings or the attachment, need or expected outcome we have. Every encounter we have with others is an opportunity in disguise, and it is through our triggers that we are alerted to witness each experience through the lens of awareness. This gives us opportunities that allow us to fully examine the three aspects of each experience in each present moment and transform any outcome into a greater benefit for all.

It is never about "out there." ALL is within you, and you seduce ALL with your own perception, viewing through your own unique inner lens.

RECOGNIZING OUR PATTERNS

The Three Aspects of the Experience

MAKING IT PERSONAL

Exercise:

From a place of awareness, *notice how any confusion or conflict will become clear the moment you become the observer of what is happening, allowing you to actually witness your own developmental programming and how it affects your response as well as the response you get from the others. When you are observing, be sure to do so from the point of genuine curiosity about yourself and others.* No Judgment!

Be sure to view all three aspects of the experience: the experience itself, you in the experience, and the processing of the experience.

REFLECTION

Observing ourselves in the process of Awareness can be irritating, and at times, quite disorienting. Anger strikes, our hands are sweaty, our heart beats faster, and our face goes red. However, with the shift to Awareness, and the practice of mindfulness, we do not judge anything— not ourselves, not the others—we simply observe. Choose to simply watch, listen, and remain curious instead of blaming and reacting.

ASK YOURSELF:

What do I believe about myself that makes me so upset, and where did I get this belief from?

What is my strength towards embracing new possibilities?

_____

_____

_____

What is my weakness when it comes to conflict?

_____

_____

_____

Do I live my life based on what is external to my being, or do I live life from what is within me and express my true self to the outside world?

_____

_____

_____

How do I use self-control to avoid being confrontational and avoid projecting my beliefs and perspectives onto others?

_____

_____

_____

As the observer, ask yourself the following:

Did I suspend all criticizing?

_____

_____

_____

Was I aware of the nature of the experience?

_____

_____

_____

Did I stay free from unhealthy attachments?

_____

_____

_____

Looking at how you and the other(s) are processing the experience, ask yourself:

Did I see anything within my own behavior that may have contributed to mine or the other's reactions to the experience?

_____

_____

_____

What might I have done differently in the experience that may have resulted in a different outcome?

_____

_____

_____

How did the other's behavioral reactions inform me?

_____

_____

_____

Why did they act in a prescribed way?

_____

_____

_____

How were they dealing with the experience differently from me?

_____

_____

_____

How did the other's behavior and decision-making affect me in this experience?

_____

_____

_____

Could I simply accept the differences?

_____

_____

_____

HAVE FUN JOURNALING

Begin a journal about your experience with Awareness and how you felt from the observer's point of view as you witnessed the experience.

Write down what you were able to witness in each aspect of the experience.

Describe the experience itself and what it was about:

_____

_____

_____

Next, describe you in the experience. What were you doing?

_____

_____

_____

Did you get triggered by the experience?

_____

_____

_____

How did you react to the trigger?

_____

_____

_____

What, if any, emotions came up for you?

_____

_____

_____

How did that make you feel?

_____

_____

_____

Do you recognize any of your patterns? If so, what were they?

_____

_____

_____

How did the other(s) react within the experience?

_____

_____

_____

Did they also get triggered?

_____

_____

_____

What might they have been feeling?

_____

_____

_____

What might you have done or said differently if you were given the opportunity to have this same experience again?

_____

_____

_____

CONNECT WITH OTHERS

Start a conversation with a friend or loved one sharing your experience with Awareness and your insights from your journaling.

Practice active listening while encouraging the other person to tell their story of an experience they were having, and share how Awareness might work for them.

While reflecting with your friend or partner on both stories, discuss any missed opportunities or any resistance to stepping into Awareness. As the observer, talk about any feelings or conclusions you had and any needs, attachments or beliefs you had that might have interfered with using the Awareness process.

Milestones

It takes a lot of practice to step into Awareness quickly when we are triggered and to remain open to intense emotions without acting out our habitual responses of defending our views or territory. By staying open, we can relax in the midst of emotional upheaval and appreciate it for what it is. How we experience this openness depends on how aware we are.

When dancing with life from the place of Awareness, there is no urge to leave the dance floor. Instead, we remain present with the intensity of the experience along with the triggers, emotions and patterns. This is even if we wish it were gone and the situation was resolved in some other way. We need to hold a space for ourselves to complete the experience fully.

Celebrate that you are now able to remain present with the experience and accept and work with uncertainty, fully attentive to your feelings, the feelings of others, and the experience itself, and sensing what is needed with an open mind and heart. Celebrate these milestones of processing all your experiences through Awareness. It is a process that leads us to consciously respond and take action from the heart.

Meditation

Sit quietly, relax and take several deep breaths while scanning your body for any areas of tension, releasing it as you go.

Now, turn your awareness inward to "see" the truth. It is the pathway to intuition, knowledge and wisdom. If you have a question regarding a choice you would like to make, and you want to access your wise guidance, ask now for wisdom regarding this situation. Feel comfort now knowing that all is well and let this ease any fears you may have.

Continue with your meditation considering how Awareness works in your life. What are the beliefs you hold onto to reflect your sense of self? If you are willing to release old, worn ideas and re-form better ones about yourself, your new awareness will reflect your new thinking. Create new beliefs about your power, beauty and intelligence that make you worthy and claim a life and joy and happiness for yourself right now.

Take a moment now to acknowledge: "My spirit is eternal." Listen carefully to your words as you take them into your heart. Feel your heart space become free from any sense of illusions that you may have towards being perfect to experience happiness and wholeness. Know that you are good, whole, beautiful and worthy of all—especially of love—simply because you are a child of the Universe.

IV

THE CRITICAL VOICE... THE WRITING
ON OUR WALL

There is no longer any doubt about the strong connection between the Writing on Our Walls and the way Life shows up for us. This brings us to the fundamental concept upon which our work is built. It is of critical importance and underlines just about every idea we are going to explore.

We Create Our Own Reality Based on the Writing on Those Walls

This statement should be tattooed on the insides of our eyelids so that we see it every time we blink. Its truth is undeniable, yet so subtle that we tend to ignore it.

We all have different words on our walls. That's why we appear to have different limits. Your limits are different than the limits of others because the truths written on your wall are different than the truths written on others… but what if they were not truths at all?

What if we were to stop and reality test this writing?

The truth is, they are just guidelines and strategies we have adopted for getting through life. Some of them are even childhood survival skills, and many of them are fiction. They are hand-me-down beliefs that were written on our walls by others, and we have been dutifully obeying them ever since.

The writing on our walls is our most prominent advisor, and we consult it all day long.

The writing on our walls represents every experience we have ever had. It contains all of our "how to's." It contains our cans and our can'ts, as well as our shoulds and our should nots. It contains our musts and our must not's. It contains our version of proper behavior as well as what we consider right or wrong in this world. It contains our judgments, our successes and our failures.

It's all there—everything we hold to be true—it's written on our walls.

Whose is the voice you listen to most in a day? Your partner's? Your child's? Does it belong to your boss?

For most of us, the voice we most listen to is our own.

When that voice is critical, as it so often is, it says things like: "You are not good enough," "You are stupid," "They will find you out," "No one could love you," and "You are a failure."

If you recognize any of those as a regular message you get from your critical voice, make a note of it because it's the Writing on **YOUR** Wall. The writing on our wall is repeated to us by our critical voice, and therefore it will be a useful clue in our discovery process. We want to know what is written on our wall.

If you feel you do not have a critical voice, there are several possibilities:

- Do you make sure you are too busy to hear it?

- Do you fail to recognize it as a critical voice because to you it is just the truth?

- Do you really believe that you are not good enough, are stupid, unlovable or a failure?

- You may experience some kind of sensation that serves the same purpose for you—a feeling or anxiety or dread, perhaps.

- You might be feeling a message somewhere in your body rather than one that is delivered in words.

Before Self Discovery:

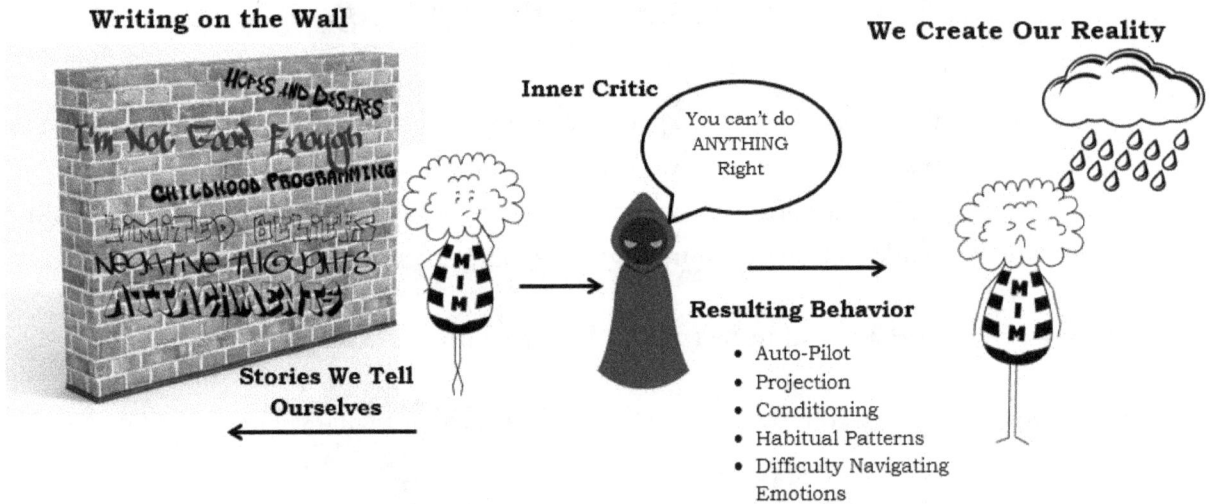

Writing on the Wall

HOPES AND DESIRES
I'm Not Good Enough
CHILDHOOD PROGRAMMING
LIMITED BELIEFS
NEGATIVE THOUGHTS
ATTACHMENTS

Stories We Tell Ourselves

Inner Critic

You can't do ANYTHING Right

We Create Our Reality

Resulting Behavior

- Auto-Pilot
- Projection
- Conditioning
- Habitual Patterns
- Difficulty Navigating Emotions

ENERGY LEVELS AND NEURON BUNDLES

At an energy level, every thought, including the thought the voice is expressing, creates a field of energy. We are beginning to understand that brain cells act as communities—they link up and work together in networks. The more we think a particular thought, the more this network builds itself and strengthens. In an hour, the synaptic connections, which are the links between the cells by which they communicate, can double. The thought expressed in the recurring critical voice is constantly building its neural muscle.

But **the good news** about that is that when we don't use a network, it withers away. Billions of neurons get busy tearing apart a network that seems no longer needed. We rewire ourselves constantly on the basis of what we pay attention to. When we stop paying attention to a critical voice, we actually change the connections in our brains. Another bit of good news from the hard science front is that we have, on average, ten times as many "neuro bundles" going from our brains to our senses as we do from our senses to our brains.

We imagine we see the world as it is. We don't. We see it as we are. We tell our senses what information we want them to collect. So, when we stop hearing the voice saying, "I am not good enough," we change the way our brains send messages to our senses to go look for evidence to prove that.

When the critical voice reveals itself, our self-discovery work is looking for connections to some of our core issues. It's important to ask yourself: "What does that feeling remind me of? When have I had this feeling before and what was my experience?"

When working with the critical voice and the writing on our walls, **"we must accept what we want to change."** Not accepting that we have a particular emotion, desire or fear is a major obstacle towards transforming or changing it. We cannot change something that we deny exists. Thus, the first step towards any change or transformation is to accept ourselves exactly as we are with all of our weaknesses, fears, attachments and desires. We need to feel that we are worthy of love and acceptance exactly as we are.

The Story

Dialogue with the Heart

"What are you afraid of?" the man asked his heart.

The heart didn't reply.

"There is no one out there that will hurt you; I'll protect you. I have grown, I am strong now, you have nothing to fear."

Still, the heart did not reply.

"Tell me, heart. Was it our father? Was it our brothers? Was it one of our lovers? None of that matters now, I am grown, no one can do anything to us."

The heart remained quiet… closed.

The man grew frustrated. "Heart, you are a coward. Maybe you are defective. Maybe I just don't have a heart that works properly. No wonder I can't feel love."

The heart closed even tighter.

For many years the man walked around, falling ever deeper into despair about his defective heart. Then one day the man grew very quiet. Quiet enough that he thought he could almost hear a whisper coming from his heart. He asked with all the compassion he was capable of, "Heart, what are you afraid of?"

The heart whispered back, "You. I'm afraid of you."

The man cried. He had protected his heart from everyone but the one person that could hurt it the most—the critic within.

To reach our inner knowledge, we need only keep processing our thoughts and feelings through our heart. When we are able to process the clichés and banality of the mind through the heart, we will find concepts of self that feel both familiar and new.

EXPERIENCE

Your Inner Critic

We experience our Inner Critic through the process of self-observation, which can be facilitated in three basic ways:

1. **Remain curious and patient** in your personal discovery process. Do not reject anything that comes up for you. Do not judge anything that comes up. Just witness and record your findings and feelings. Try to discover your beliefs and where they might have come from, and once again, do this without judgment. Remember that those caregivers that wrote on your wall also had others back through time that wrote on theirs. **People do what they do based on the writing on their walls.**

2. **Keep a daily journal.** Our observations will be much clearer and more fruitful if they are written down on paper. When we simply observe mentally, there is ample room for contradictions to coexist and details to slip by. Sometimes our problems breed in the confusion of unclear emotions and thoughts. Writing down our thoughts can help us to perceive our personalities much more clearly. In this daily journal, we can keep a record of the major emotional experiences and thoughts we experience each day. In this way, we will gradually uncover the basic emotional patterns that we have repeatedly created in our lives. We can then analyze the inner causes of these experiences, and record daily the major positive and negative emotions. Once a month we can set aside a special time to read through what we have observed to draw conclusions and make some decisions about what we would like to do to improve our reality.

3. **Work with the questionnaires** in this workbook for more objective self-analysis. In later sections, we will discuss some penetrating questions which will help us discover the attachments, aversions, fears, goals, values, talents and inclinations which motivate our thoughts, words and actions, and thus create our reality.

DIALOGUE

Know your Inner Voice

Christina Reeves:

Most of us have a very limited "intimate" contact with the voice in our head. By ignoring it and maintaining our habitual patterns, we are deadening ourselves to our inner world. An honest examination of these recurring conversations and the patterns or the way they make us feel—the way we react to our emotions and the way we think in terms of rigid belief systems—is the way to quiet the mind. By becoming intimate with our inner voice, we can learn a lot about ourselves.

Dimitrios Spanos:

Yes, Christina, like the outer world, our inner world is complex and has the capacity to handle myriads of thoughts, memories and feelings about these thoughts and memories. Our inner world is a mixture of conscious, subconscious and unconscious thoughts and beliefs all synthesized to create our outer world. Within this network, each and every word and feeling has its own energy, and no matter how tiny each of our thoughts or feelings are, they will affect our lives. Our mind works in a fascinating way and uses the brain's hundreds of billions of nerve cells at incredible speeds to process images, thoughts and feelings, and communicates to us the messages written on our walls. Our inner critical voice simply propels the existence of past memories and/ or any future anxiety we may have.

RECOGNIZING OUR PATTERNS

Thanking the Critical Voice

MAKING IT PERSONAL

It is important to realize that the critical voice has a number of upsides, the first of which is that it is actually on our side. Whatever it says to us and however unfriendly it sounds, it is almost certainly trying to help in some way. It is telling us what is written on our walls and sometimes even why we adhere to our old patterns of behavior.

For example, if it says, "We are not good enough," it is as well for us to know that so we don't make ourselves more vulnerable than we need to be. Or if it says, "You don't belong," it might believe it is keeping you safe by making sure you do not try to be included in a group it thinks might reject you and hurt you. It might be trying to keep you safe by reminding you not to try. So instead of criticizing it back, fighting it, or trying to silence it, we can start by thanking the critical voice for what it has been trying to do for us and use it to help us in a different way.

THE WISDOM OF GANDHI

Did You Know?

What we believe creates our reality, and just like Gandhi says, "Our beliefs become our thoughts, our thoughts become our words, our words become actions, our actions become habits, our habits become our values and our values become our destiny."

EXERCISE

The following questions are not always easy to answer, and many beginners at this process of self-discovery feel frustrated. My suggestion is to try turning this frustration into genuine curiosity about getting to know yourself and others on a deeper level. Play with the mystery and wonder of all that is, and remember, this is a process of discovery of self!

Ask yourself these questions:

Do I hear/pay attention to the voice in my head?

_____

_____

_____

How often do I hear the voice in my head?

_____

_____

_____

What is it saying to me?

_____

_____

_____

Is it positive or critical?

_____

_____

_____

Are these negative statements? What are they?

_____

_____

_____

Are they positive statements? What are those?

_____

_____

_____

Is what the voice is saying ringing true or false? Reality test what the voice is saying.

_____

_____

_____

What do you think about what it says?

_____

_____

_____

Do you believe in what the voice is saying?

_____

_____

_____

Which statements do you concur with?

_____

_____

_____

Which statements do you not concur with?

_____

_____

_____

What emotions come up for you when you hear the voice in your head?

_____

_____

_____

Does it sound like someone you might have heard before—perhaps a caregiver?

_____

_____

_____

How does what it says make you feel? Name the emotions.

_____

_____

_____

REFLECTION

> **Once we begin the journey of self-discovery, we never turn back. We cannot "un-know" something we have discovered.** We embark on a mission to find our authentic self and create a new map of our mind. The previous programming of the mind becomes obsolete, and soon we begin to open the door to our destiny.

Reflect on the following questions:

- What defines me and who am I?

- Am I the sum of previous beliefs, conclusions, and a reflection of my needs, wants, and reactions?

- Or do I have a different purpose in life?

- Am I the image of a personality developed over the years through a web of old beliefs, thoughts and emotions stored in a memory bank, or a universal creation of new ideas, hopes, and dreams?

- Take a moment to reflect on your inner voice. What does this voice say to you about yourself?

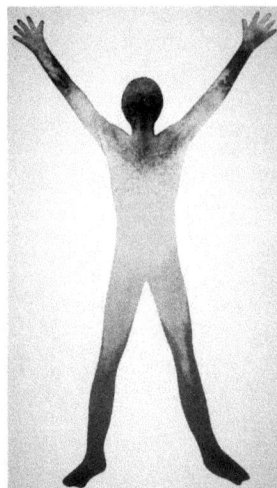

ASK YOURSELF:

In what ways does your inner critic keep following the same thoughts and patterns from the sub-conscious and unconscious levels?

_____

_____

_____

What kind of language does your inner critic use when influenced by the emotion of fear or doubt?

_____

_____

_____

When you hear the voice, is fear operating in your body and your life?

_____

_____

_____

Which of your childhood wounds continue to impact your life making you feel unsafe?

_____

_____

_____

How does your inner critic interpret various situations?

_____

_____

_____

Are these situations really threatening or just a mental creation?

_____

_____

_____

How flexible are you towards changing your current mind chatter, inner thoughts and beliefs?

_____

_____

_____

How might you transform a completely new inner sense of yourself by turning your inner critic into your Champion?

_____

_____

_____

HAVE FUN JOURNALING

Begin a journal about your experience with the voice in your head, reality test what the voice says, and try to capture the details it says and record it. Go ahead and respond to the voice and tell the voice how you feel, noting both your emotions and reactions.

Use this journal entry as a running journal—a tool to record everything the voice says to you. What the voice is saying is a good indicator of the writing on your wall. We want to know in our discovery process what is written on the wall, but remember: this writing is not who you are—it's someone else's story! Make notes of any disagreements or conflicts you feel with what the voice has to say.

Once again, be prepared not to have all the questions or answers—remain open. Rather than try to solve all the problems, allow time to process and allow more questions to come up. Remember that it is often best to complete the journal entry with a question rather than an answer.

CONNECT WITH OTHERS

Start a conversation with a friend or loved one, sharing your experience with the voice in your head and your insights from your journaling.

Practice active listening while encouraging the other person to tell their story of how the voice in their head shows up for them.

As you reflect with your friend or partner on both the experiences and the stories, discuss any conflicts or reactions either of you had to what the voice said.

Discuss any missed opportunities to feeling things fully and how any needs, attachments or beliefs you might have had that interfered with (or even supported) the voice.

Milestones

*Most of us have a very limited "intimate" contact with the
voice in our head. By ignoring it and maintaining our habitual
patterns, we are deadening ourselves to our inner world.*

*An honest examination of these recurring conversations and the patterns or
the way they make us feel—the way we react to our emotions and the way
we think in terms of rigid belief systems—is the way to quiet the mind.*

*By becoming intimate with our inner voice, we can learn a lot about
ourselves. Through the practice of monitoring the inner voice, we learn
to recognize and experience ourselves more directly, coming to know more
and more intimately why we do what we do or think what we think.*

*Be sure to celebrate the courage and honesty required to look at
what lies underneath what the voice is saying and witness the
discovery of how your thoughts continuously create your reality.*

*Celebrate your ability to constantly create change and
dismantle the critical voice as you learn to experience what's
written on your walls in a gentle, loving way.*

Self Realization:

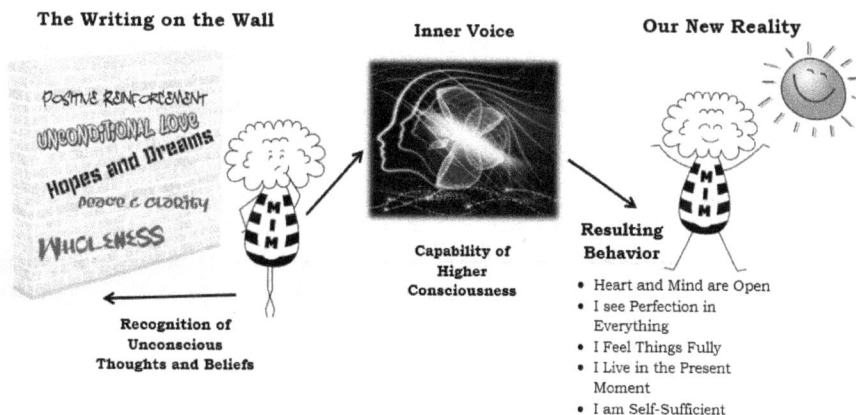

The Writing on the Wall

POSITIVE REINFORCEMENT
UNCONDITIONAL LOVE
Hopes and Dreams
PEACE & CLARITY
WHOLENESS

**Recognition of
Unconscious
Thoughts and Beliefs**

Inner Voice

**Capability of
Higher
Consciousness**

Our New Reality

**Resulting
Behavior**

- Heart and Mind are Open
- I see Perfection in
  Everything
- I Feel Things Fully
- I Live in the Present
  Moment
- I am Self-Sufficient

Meditation

Sit quietly, relax and take several deep breaths while scanning your body for any areas of tension. Release that tension by breathing deeply into those areas.

- *As you sit in meditation, reflect on the power of your mind and how you use it for your good.*

- *Do you fill your mind with information, or do you seek knowledge and wisdom about the higher truths of life?*

- *Do you think thoughts that support your happiness, or ones that punish and belittle your spirit?*

- *Can you find joy and ease in self-acceptance, love for yourself and appreciation for your life just as it is?*

- *Know that you are a gift to the world and think loving, good thoughts about yourself now.*

Remember, the voice is trying to assist you by showing you any limitations you might have. Feel the palpable and overriding nature of the factual errors expressed by the critical voice and its impact on your life experiences. Feel the complete absence of evidence, as the information coming from the critical voice is based on old programming.

- *Do you want to experience bliss?*

- *Are you willing to live your life in that state now?*

Your work is to have sufficient trust and substantial faith coupled with the deep experience that you are loved to allow this to unfold. It takes commitment, wisdom and love.

Think of a beautiful memory that stands out in your mind; anything that touched your soul and remember the feeling you experienced when you had that experience. Allow yourself to be transported to this place where you were touched by this beauty, and take that experience into your heart space. Allow it to soften your heart and keep your spirit fueled. Allow this beautiful memory to shine its light on your world.

In this moment, there is only peace. There is beauty all around you, bliss within you, and you feel serene and calm. Nothing can destroy this feeling; you are anchored in the truth of who you are. Choose this place, this space whenever you wish to rest in peace and tranquility.

V

EMOTIONAL INTELLIGENCE

...Is Living Mindfully through the Heart

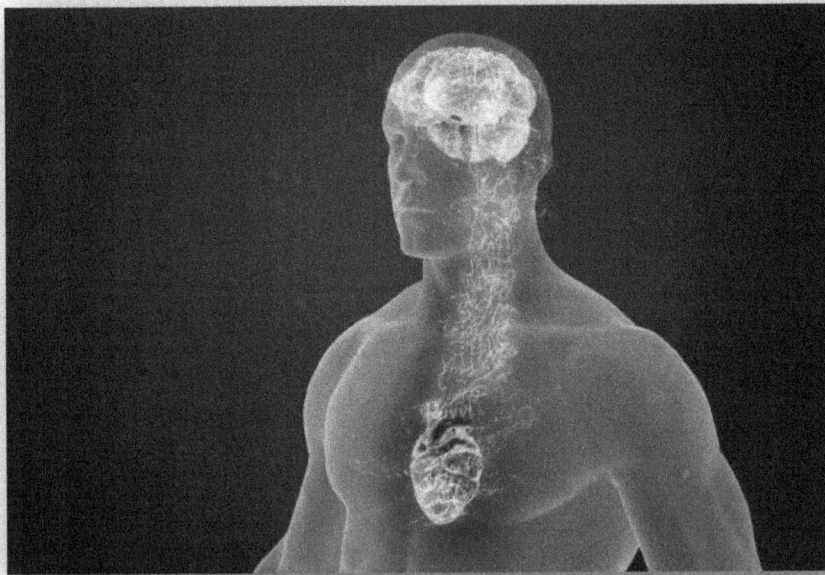

WHAT IS EMOTIONAL INTELLIGENCE?

Emotional Intelligence is what makes us tick. **We observe and identify** our emotions and thoughts and recognize our patterns. We use our discernment and wisdom to generate more choices. We turn possibilities and opportunities to personal realities.

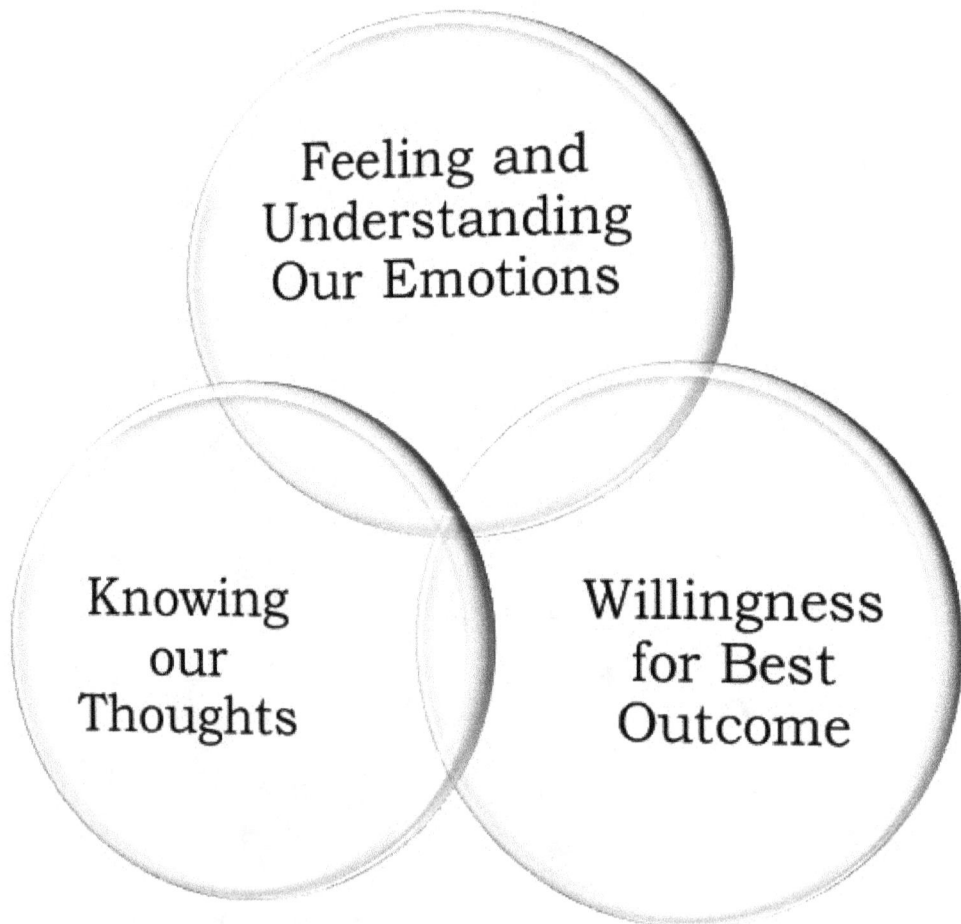

Feeling and
Understanding
Our Emotions

Knowing
our
Thoughts

Willingness
for Best
Outcome

Cultivating Emotional Intelligence is one of the most powerful ways to transform our lives by becoming consciously aware of our beliefs and feelings about ourselves.

RECOGNIZING OUR EMOTIONS

All emotions play a role in modifying our thoughts, behaviors and actions. This means that even experiencing "negative" emotions from time to time, such as anger or sadness, can be part of a normal and healthy functioning mind. In the same way, as pain motivates us to take our hand off of a hot stove, negative emotions are signals in our nervous system telling us how to adapt to our environment.

Our emotions have a variety of functions in improving the way we respond to our environment. These functions are to:

- Direct attention toward stimuli in our environment that may be important.

- Enhance learning and memory of events which are emotionally significant.

- Guide behaviors in response to how we feel.

- Improve social interaction by communicating our emotions and understanding the emotions of others.

- Drive moral development by providing us with compassion toward the well-being of ourselves and others.

The practice of Emotional Intelligence teaches us the ability to recognize and understand emotions in ourselves and others, and the use of this knowledge affects how we manage behavior, navigate social complexities and make personal decisions that achieve positive results.

Emotional intelligence is about personal competence of our self-awareness and self-management skills and focuses more on you individually than on your interactions with other people. It focuses on your ability to self-manage and remain aware of your emotions and your behavior tendencies, perceiving them accurately as they happen while remaining flexible to positively direct your behavior.

Our emotions can and do **drive our behavior** and impact people, either positively or negatively. While our intellect can help us to resolve problems, make calculations or process information, emotional intelligence allows us to be more creative and use our emotions to resolve our problems.

The Story

A Glass of Water

A trainer walked around a room while teaching stress management to an audience. As she did so, she raised a glass of water. Everyone expected they'd be asked the old "half empty or half full" question. Instead, she asked, "How heavy is this glass of water?"

The answers ranged from 8 oz to 16 oz.

She replied, "The absolute weight doesn't matter. What's important is how long I hold it. If I hold it for a minute, it's not heavy. If I hold it for an hour, I'll have an ache in my arm. If I hold it for a day, my arm will be numb and feel paralysed. In each case, the weight of the glass doesn't change but, the longer I hold it, the heavier it becomes."

She continued, "The stresses and worries in life are like that glass of water. Think about them for a while and nothing happens. Think about them a bit longer and they begin to hurt. And if you think about them all day long, you will feel paralysed—incapable of doing anything."

It's important to remember to let go of your stresses. Put your burdens down when you can. Don't carry them for hours and days and months.

Remember to put down the glass!

SURFING THROUGH LIFE

People with high Emotional Intelligence generally find that they have an extra dose of curiosity. This curiosity adds to improved responsiveness, as well as increases in quality of life, effectiveness and decision-making. It's like a muscle that can be learned and strengthened. People with high Emotional Intelligence are self-aware, self-managing and self-directing. By using their willpower, they are able to direct their lives with appropriate responses in all their experiences and to the people they're interacting with.

Curiosity = Improved Responsiveness
→ Quality of Life
→ Effectiveness
→ Love and Relationships
→ Well-Being

EXPERIENCE

When you use Emotional Intelligence, your energy flows freely. You're more flexible, balanced and creative. You view yourself and the world with more compassion and understanding. You have more energy and are open to new possibilities. You have all the power you could possibly need to create a new reality—a reality of vibrant health and wellbeing. Here are a few tips to acting with Emotional Intelligence:

- Be passionate about your life and the experiences you fill it with.

- Remain open to as much input as possible.

- Don't shut down the feedback loop with judgment, rigid beliefs and prejudices.

- Don't censor incoming data through denial.

- Examine other points of view as if they were your own.

- Take responsibility for making conscious choices.

- Work on psychological blocks like shame and guilt—they falsely color your reality.

- Free yourself emotionally—to be emotionally resilient is the best defense against growing rigid.

- Harbor no secrets, for they create dark places in the psyche.

- Be willing to redefine yourself every day.

- Don't regret the past or fear the future. Both bring misery through self-doubt.

DIALOGUE

Why Emotional Intelligence?

Christina Reeves: Cultivating Emotional Intelligence is one of the most powerful ways to transform our lives. Developing our Emotional Intelligence muscles helps us create positive change in our personal lives and helps us improve the quality of our relationships with others. These changes will lead to higher levels of conscious engagement with our families, friends and colleagues, in our schools, our communities and even our countries. They will also contribute to a deeper understanding between nations improving the world around us.

Dimitrios Spanos:

Christina, you are right. Awareness is not enough. We need Emotional Intelligence as well. During the course of my life, I have met many intelligent and successful people, but their brilliance was more self-serving than serving others. By practicing Emotional Intelligence, every event and every outcome can be an expression of love from the Universe, giving us the opportunity to realize the truth or not. We all have free will.

RECOGNIZING OUR PATTERNS

Identifying Our Emotions

Making it Personal

There is power in the ability to name emotions. When we name feelings, we get a handle on how we are dealing with our own experiences, and then we are better able communicate more effectively with others.

Validate feelings. Name them and acknowledge them.

Start by assuming they're valuable and useful. Remember that if you don't pay attention, feelings usually escalate; what we resist persists. The earlier you attend to this message, the easier it will be to step into awareness. When strong feelings come up, simply be an observer. "Oh, that's interesting," or "What can I learn from this?" Stay curious; don't obey feelings blindly, but don't lock them away either. Find the middle ground. Feelings are just signals saying "something interesting is happening!"

Remember, there are no "good" or "bad" feelings. All of our feelings are neutral, and we simply need to become aware of them. There is no need to apologize, feel guilty or criticize ourselves or others. Just keep a curious, caring tonality.

We have a choice about how we use our emotions. Emotions are sensations, and we need to be able to distinguish between a sensation and the way people act. For example: anger is an emotion, but yelling is an action. One need not yell just because they are angry.

TAKE CONTROL OF YOUR EMOTIONS

Emotional Intelligence isn't passive. It directly leads to action (and sometimes inaction). As you take steps to expand your emotional intelligence, you will naturally find yourself harnessing your mind's infinite power to create greater health, happiness and love in your life.

EXERCISE

While a generalized approach will reduce complexity, and may work well for some people, optimal learning is personal. When it comes to a single person, we're all different, unique human beings, and whatever works for you might not work for others. Even still, one commonality is that far too often we overreact with too much emotion, or we underreact with too little emotion.

Living with Emotional Intelligence is a step forward in learning to lead and live from the heart, embracing our own feelings as a source of insight. We can welcome and embrace our feelings, even the complicated ones, as a way to understand what's going on for us and the other people in our experiences.

It's easy when the feelings are what we want, but the best learning comes when we are willing to be courageous and open enough to engage with our emotions even when they're difficult.

Emotional Intelligence is an "inside job." It begins with the foundation of an enhanced self-discovery into your unique patterns of behavior that then fuels your choices with the goal of supporting your values and purpose in living. Don't be afraid to turn inward, be curious about who you really are, then show up to support the change you wish to be in the world.

It's important to get comfortable with your emotions, especially because emotions have functions. Emotions are not just about feeling something. You want to determine:

What's the message of the emotion?

_____

_____

_____

How can we handle emotions more effectively?

_____

_____

_____

What do we need to know in order to get a handle on our feelings?

_____

_____

_____

EMOTIONAL INTELLIGENCE AND THE HEART

Imagine being a conductor of an orchestra, having the skills, talents and understanding of musical notes. After mastering the art of listening to **musical organs and their rhythmical flow**, you efficiently communicate the melodic notes to musicians and audiences, bringing harmonious music to all. Emotional Intelligence works in a similar way. But instead of working with musical notes, you work with your emotions and the emotions of others, becoming aware of the power, energy and sensitivity of each word.

LEARN HOW:

- Shift your thoughts to your heart.

- Ask yourself: how do I overcome my mind's conditioning?

It is Important to Remember...

Our heart has all of the beauty and warmth
and resonates with all that exists.

REFLECTION

Self-reflection is another step towards practicing Emotional Intelligence. Try to sit silently for a few minutes every day and practice introspection.

Create, remember and become aware of your own tales your stories are linked with particular experiences, moods, feelings and emotional states.

Notice the blends of emotions in your stories. You may experience many emotions at once. Try to identify all your emotions. When you want to change your feelings, remember the stories and the range of feelings that emerge.

Here are some tips to assist you in putting your Emotional Intelligence into action:

- Be an observer of yourself. Pay attention to what you feel and how those feelings contribute, distract, enhance or challenge you.

- Starting with self-awareness, acknowledge your emotions and where you feel them in your body.

- Become more emotionally literate. Build your emotional vocabulary. You should be able to name your emotions.

- Train yourself to sense your emotions via sensations in your body.

- While in Awareness, try to acknowledge your emotions. Think of them not as good or bad or right or wrong, but as a source of information that helps you gain self-awareness.

- Become an expert at unpacking your emotions and thinking on them. This is about stopping and asking, "Wait a minute—what's going on for me here? What am I feeling? What am I thinking? What does all this mean for me?"

- Notice your own strengths and lean into them more fully.

- Pay attention to the thoughts and feelings in the present moment. Do this with purpose, setting aside judgement, and be present as if your life depended on it.

- Step into Awareness and recognize your patterns. Notice when you set yourself up for low Emotional Intelligence moments that become patterned habitual habits.

AWARENESS

Be aware of two common traps:

1. **Passing critical judgment** on others only serves to elevate or affirm one's superiority over another person's choices or intelligence. Emotional Intelligence begins when we learn to recognize these habitual patterns and then retrain ourselves to restrain from making any negative comment about them.

2. **Taking offense** is another part of recognizing patterns, and it is a huge struggle for many of us. In today's world, we have been taught to take offense at even the most trivial matters. Taking offense and feeling offended can quickly escalate to criticism, judgment, bitterness and lack of forgiveness. You are practicing Emotional Intelligence when you notice the other person's comment or action, and instead of taking offense and taking it personally, just consider it as data. Remain only the observer!

Reaction:

Determine if any of our core values or personal boundaries are being challenged.

Does this result in an unconscious emotional response?

Action Plan:

There's a lot of discussion on the importance of focusing on strengths instead of weaknesses. Experiential Wisdom says the answer is somewhere in the middle. The fact is, something within us needs to be discovered or uncovered and that "something" needs our attention.

ASK YOURSELF:

It is through our self-discovery process where we are challenged to see, accept, and break our habitual patterns. Looking at our full range of needs, attachments and capabilities can assist us with the learning process.

Consider the following questions:

When does the most effective learning take place for you?

_____

_____

_____

What data are you able to discover that informs you about your emotions?

_____

_____

_____

What data are you able to discover related to your needs and attachments? (See the Possible Needs List in the back of this book.)

_____

_____

_____

What does it mean to you to live from the heart?

_____

_____

_____

Where might you focus your attention for growth?

_____

_____

_____

OUR GOLDEN NUGGETS

A golden nugget is an experience that is used to motivate yourself when times get tough. Think about a time in your life when your Life Force Energy was at an all-time high. Revisit this experience and write about this experience in as much detail as you can. Read it often.

What are your golden nuggets?

The Five Elements of Trust

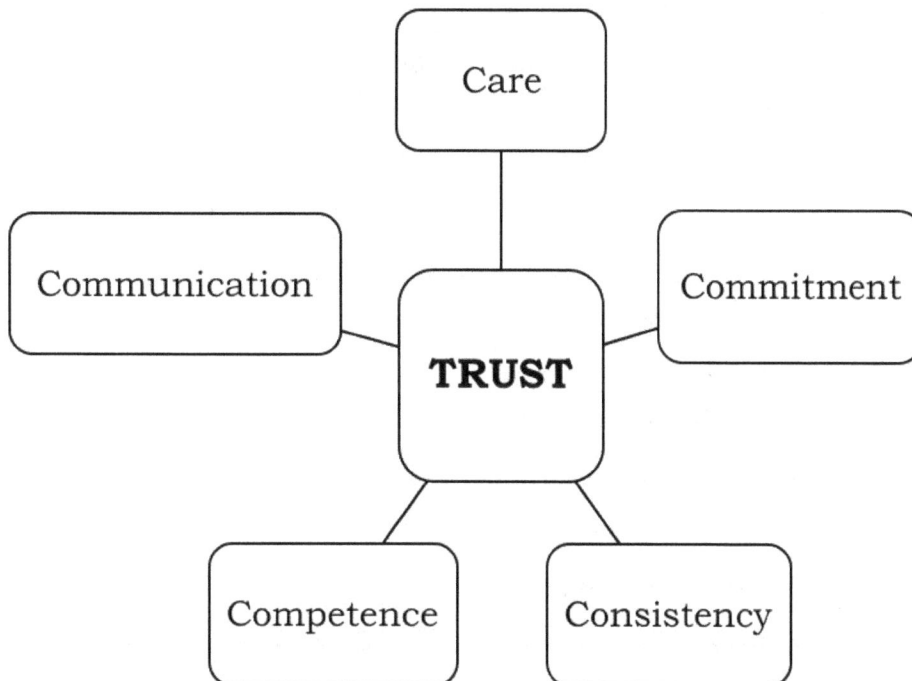

HAVE FUN JOURNALING

When engaging in anything new, especially if it involves change, you will want to increase your Awareness in the present moment. Change only happens in the NOW.

Write of a past success and include any acts of Emotional Intelligence you used to help you achieve your goal. Know that there are five elements we might consider when working with cultivating our Emotional Intelligence, shown in the graphic above. They are all related to trust. In relation to Emotional Intelligence, spend time pondering them and be sure to ask yourself what they mean to you and include these in your writing. These elements are: Commitment, Consistency, Care, Competence and Communication.

Ask yourself the following:

- *How might you use Emotional Intelligence to remove the barriers of separation and create a happy, peaceful environment for yourself and others?*

- *How might you better understand your own emotions and the emotions of others?*

- *How might you handle conflict in an easier and less stressful way?*

- *What would it take to eliminate blaming and transform any negative energy in your life?*

CONNECT WITH OTHERS

Start a conversation with a friend or loved one, sharing your experience and your insights from your journaling. Emotional Intelligence is one of the most powerful learning solutions, and it is unique and meaningful to the one learning. Remember, we all see things from our own unique perspective.

- How might you encourage and engage yourself and others to nurture great relationships and provide a network of inner support?

- How might you promote a healthy social environment for expanding ideas and creativity?

When engaging with others keep your heart and mind open, holding a space to listen to what the others have to say. Remember that, "No Way is The Way." The most powerful growth comes from an approach that's uniquely you. One-size fits none.

Milestones

Learning Emotional Intelligence is like training and fine-tuning muscles that may have never been used. The elation we feel when we have learned an important lesson, achieved a goal, or had a big breakthrough can sometimes be met with a period of downtime afterwards. During this period of transition, we may feel unsure and not know where to turn next. During the pause between achievements, many people begin to wonder what their life is truly about. These feelings are common and strike everyone from time to time.

Human beings are active creatures; we feel best when we are working on a project or vigorously pursuing a goal. But there is nothing inherently wrong with spending a day, a week, or even a month simply existing and not having a plan. Just be. It won't be long before you embark upon your next voyage of growth and discovery.

Celebrate your successes. Honoring yourself in this way is a motivator for achieving higher levels of success. As you think clearly about issues that require reflection, you will find that you are strengthening your Emotional Intelligence's muscles. Your mind is getting sharper, and you will begin to cultivate your intuition to reach higher levels of truth and knowing.

This higher knowledge will enable you to see a bigger picture and a solution. Practice Emotional Intelligence in any situation, any experience or any problem you face.

Meditation

Close your eyes, sit quietly and take several deep breaths. Let go of all the mind stuff that happened today and focus on deepening your breathing and releasing any tension you might have accumulated throughout your day. Begin reflecting on any problem that you would like to have more insight to assist you in solving it.

As you reflect about the problem, ask a question in your mind such as, "How, do I see my way forward in this experience?"

Breathe deeply and wait as you focus your attention on the perceived problem.

Accept this guidance and allow yourself to reflect on any answers you receive before you choose.

You always have a choice in what you want to understand or want to know.

Trust what you hear, and if you need more clarity, ask another question. The second question may be in regard to your first question, or it might be completely unrelated.

Listen quietly for the answer and trust that what you hear is correct. As you think clearly about issues that require reflection, you will find that you are strengthening your Emotional Intelligence muscles.

Your mind is getting sharper, and you will begin to cultivate your intuition to reach higher levels of truth and knowing. This higher knowledge will enable you to see a bigger picture and a solution.

Practice this exercise for any situation, any experience or any problem you face.

VI

THE MIND IS NOT FREE TO BE HAPPY

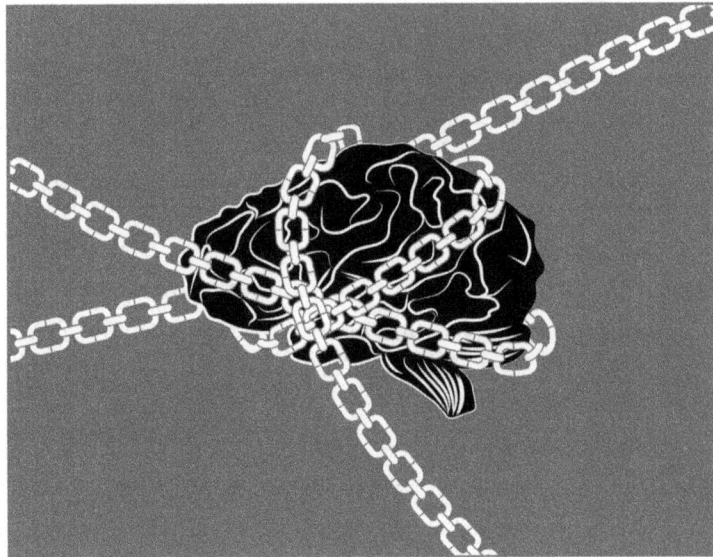

We all seek happiness, and in our search for this happiness, we attempt to create a world which we have been programmed to believe as children that we need to have in order to be happy. As we are seldom able to perfectly create this ideal world which would supposedly supply us with unlimited happiness, we are seldom satisfied with our lives.

THE SEARCH FOR HAPPINESS

This search for happiness is based on the hope of our finding stable and preferably unchanging sources of security, pleasure, affirmation and unconditional love in our external world. We seek especially to satisfy those needs which have been left unfulfilled in our past. Our unhappiness comes from our wants, attachments, needs and expectations. When we are attached to our wants and needs in order to feel safe, worthy and free, then we feel more frequently hurt and angry.

When we have wants, needs and expectations, we tend to push and pull the Life Force Energy in an attempt to force a particular outcome that we have become attached to. To accomplish the outcome in our favor, we might find our self totally ignoring the perspectives of others, or we might engage in some attempts to manipulate the outcome to fit our needs. Then if our needs do not get met, we tend to go into overwhelm and overreact to the circumstances that we ourselves created!

Sometimes we become attached to specific persons, objects, situations, positions and roles in an attempt to feel that we have secured our needs. We fight to obtain what we need. If we do not achieve what we believe we need, we feel that we are a failure, perhaps becoming depressive if we feel impotent to obtain what we desire. Or we may become bitter and angry towards those who have "obstructed" us from or "cheated" us out of what we need.

We often develop positive feelings towards those who help us obtain what we "need," and negative feelings towards those who obstruct us. We harbor jealousy towards those who have what we need, and we fear those who might take what we need from us.

We may fear losing what we have, and we spend much energy trying to protect what we have. The more we feel we need, the more energy we lose in trying to obtain, sustain and protect what we believe we need. These attachments become the cause of our conflicts with others. Our relationships with family, friends and coworkers become strained because we frequently fear that their behavior embodies some type of danger for us and that some of our needs will not be fulfilled.

THE SEARCH FOR HAPPINESS

SURFACE HAPPINESS

Conditional Happiness is derived from:

- Material Objects
- People Around You
- Fleeting Experiences

The Story

The 99 Club

Once upon a time, there lived a man that could be neither driven nor wiled. This puzzled the King who, despite his life of luxury, was neither happy nor content. Why was he, the Ruler of the Land with so much wealth, unhappy and miserable?

One day, the King came upon a servant who was singing happily while he worked. The King asked the servant, "Why are you so happy?" The man replied, "My Lord, I am nothing but a servant, but my family and I don't need too much, just a roof over our heads, a place to sleep and warm food to fill our bellies."

Later on that day, the unsatisfied King sought the advice of his most trusted advisor. After hearing the King's story about his encounter with the servant, the advisor replied, "Awe my King, I believe that the servant has not been made part of The 99 Club."

"And what exactly is The 99 Club?" asked the King.

The advisor replied, "Your Majesty, to truly understand what The 99 Club is, you must put 99 gold coins in a bag and leave it on the doorstep of the servant."

So, the King ordered that this be done. When the servant arose in the morning, he saw the bag. When he opened the bag, he shouted out in joy, "So many gold coins!"

He began to count them. After a few counts, he was satisfied that there were 99 coins. However, he was a bit puzzled about what happened to that last gold coin. "Surely, no one would leave 99 coins, they would leave 100!" He thought. He looked everywhere he could, but could not find that final coin. So, he decided to work harder than ever to earn that missing gold coin.

From that day, the servant was no longer happy. He was overworked, tired, grumpy and angry with his family for not helping him make that 100th gold coin. He even stopped singing while he worked.

> *Seeing this change in the servant, the King was puzzled. Once again, he sought his advisor's help. The advisor said, "Your Majesty, the servant has now officially joined The 99 Club."*
>
> *He continued, "The 99 Club is a name given to people who have plenty to be happy about, but are never content; always yearning and striving for that something extra. These people tell themselves, 'Let me get that one final thing, or if only I could have this or that and then I will be happy for life.'"*

Moral of the Story: we can be happy, even with very little in our lives, but the minute we're given something bigger and better, we want even more! We lose our sleep and our happiness, we hurt the people around us… all these as a price for our growing needs and desires. We must learn to maintain a balance of our need and desires to enjoy a happy life with what we already have.

EXPECTATION IS THE ROOT OF SUFFERING

Did You Know?

> *No thing and no one are right/wrong or good/bad. However, our attachment to them will create suffering whenever we cannot have our desired outcome.*

EXPERIENCE

MANAGING OUR NEEDS AND ATTACHMENTS

We all have basic needs, and most of our needs can be listed in one or more categories. Our happiness and our emotional harmony depend on how we recognize and manage our needs.

First, we must **learn to diminish the strength of our needs** so that they are transformed from attachments to preferences. When we are attached to something, we are unhappy when we cannot have it, and we fear losing it when we have it. When we *prefer* something, we are happy when we have it, but can also be happy if we do not. We are not overcome with anxiety with the fear of losing when we have it.

Second, we must **become more adept at fulfilling our needs** so that there is not such a great gap between what we want and what we have.

Third, we must **attend to the evolution of our needs**. It is natural that in a process of evolution, our needs will gradually change if we allow them to. Needs and desires are the natural powers of nature which move us in various directions. As spiritual evolution is the purpose of all creation, our needs and desires will lead us in that direction if we allow them to evolve naturally. For example; as children, we naturally lose our desire for dolls and toy cars. We naturally mature out of our need for our mother and father to be with us continually. In the same way, it is only natural for the mother to stop needing to play that role when her children no longer need a mother. If she continued playing the role—not letting go of that need, which has naturally lost its usefulness in her life purpose—it would be painful for both her and the child.

DIALOGUE

Happiness

Christina Reeves:

By participating fully in life, welcoming our human idiosyncrasies, fear as well as the safety, sorrow as well as bliss, even shame as well as pride, and by using all of our emotions as advisors and signals, we will find ourselves on an adventure to live life fully. In the end, unhappiness will seem like a phantom, something barely remembered. We will no longer limit ourselves to the pursuit of happiness; we will become the happiness we have been seeking..

Dimitrios Spanos:

The Greek philosopher, Aristotle, used the word Eudaimonia to describe happiness. Eudaimonia is the experience of our guardian spirit of joy in life. Life is beautiful, graceful and marvelous. We are all gifted with precious gifts, a marvelous mind, an incredible body, and a warm, loving and cosmic heart. Just like Nature that uses its forces to bring all the elements into equilibrium, we need to bring our precious gifts of life, body, mind, heart and soul into perfect alignment. We must learn to live within the sacred rhythms of our loving heart that rise from the depths of our soul in silence and stillness.

RECOGNIZING OUR PATTERNS

Attachments and Unhappiness

Making it Personal

TYPES OF ATTACHMENTS

The words addiction and attachment refer to any needs we have pertaining to any object, person, experience, role, quality or even idea that we believe we cannot be happy without. Unhappiness ensues when we do not have that particular thing we are attached to.

We might be addicted to:

- receiving another's attention
- being accepted
- being loved exclusively
- being cared for and protected by others
- possessing power over others
- being rejected
- pursuing professional success
- being the prettiest or the smartest
- being spiritual

- being right
- maintaining order and/or cleanliness
- acquiring money and material possessions
- being the victim
- being in control
- being better than others
- being strong
- being weak
- and many other possibilities

EXERCISE

A CHOICE:

When we are attached to something we have not yet been able to manifest, we have two choices.

1. We can **suffer** because we cannot get the outcome or object we want, and thus get trapped in a vicious circle of suffering and unhappiness.

2. We can allow our attachment to become a **preference** which we will enjoy having but can live without. A good example of this is when we become attached to acceptance, approval or love from a specific person, such as a parent, spouse or child. When we cannot get their affirmation, we feel hurt and angry. We are so focused on that which we cannot get that we are blind to what is offered so abundantly to us from other sources.

REFLECTION

The only difference between our happiness and our suffering is not the way things are in the moment, but rather our response to the moment. It's our acceptance or rejection of the moment and what is arising now. Imagine how different and happier our life would be if we did this one simple thing.

Simply put, **we cannot accept what life is offering us.** As we often do not have the power to change the world or the people around us, we are inclined to become unhappy, depressed, angry, jealous, fearful, hateful, bitter, etc. It is important to remember that it is not the life event that causes our negative feelings, but rather our addictive programming which prevents us from accepting that which we cannot change.

ATTACHMENTS OR PREFERENCES

We do have a choice. We can change our attachments into preferences. We can prefer something to happen, but if it doesn't, we can accept that and be happy without it. This does not mean we should not try to change whatever we can in accordance with the way we prefer things to be, but while we do this, we must accept the ultimate result.

This is a practical solution that needs to be employed once we have done everything within our power to improve our external circumstances. **The only lasting way to find inner peace and happiness is to change our internal programming.**

Remembering the following prayer by St. Francis will help:

"Lord help me to change what I can, to accept what I cannot, and to know the difference between the two."

ASK YOURSELF:

When we are unhappy, we often feel conflicted within. This conflict represents incongruences between what we think in our mind and what our heart knows.

Play with the mystery and wonder of all that is by asking yourself the following:

What makes me happy?

_____

_____

_____

What makes me unhappy?

_____

_____

_____

What is it that is actually bothering me, triggering my unhappiness?

_____

_____

_____

What do I feel?

_____

_____

_____

What are the emotions that I feel at this moment?

_____

_____

_____

What do I believe consciously or subconsciously about myself or others which is causing me to feel unhappy?

_____

_____

_____

What may have happened in the past which may have programmed me to believe these beliefs and are now causing my pain or unhappiness?

_____

_____

_____

HAVE FUN JOURNALING

Begin a journal about your experience with happiness. Write about a moment in time when you felt happy. Write what you feel might have contributed to your happiness and describe the emotions you felt. It is helpful to use the emotions list in the appendices in the back of this book to capture all of them.

Next, write about your experience with unhappiness. Try to determine what you might have felt that caused or contributed to that experience and attempt to identify all the emotions you felt.

Are you in touch with what happiness means to you?

Ask yourself daily if you are feeling happy. If not, why not?

We want to get more specific when describing our happiness by using words that accurately describe our happiness.

List all the experiences you've had that contributed to your current state of happiness.

Be prepared not to have all the questions or answers—remain open. End the journal entry with a question and the mind will continue to process the experience and the question.

CONNECT WITH OTHERS

Start a conversation with a friend or loved one, sharing your experiences of both happiness and unhappiness and your insights from your journaling.

Actively listen while encouraging the other person to tell their story of where they are on the happiness scale and why.

When reflecting with your friend or partner on both stories, discuss any missed opportunities to feeling profound happiness.

Discuss how needs, attachments or beliefs might have interfered with that happiness.

Milestones

Take a moment to sink into your happiness and feel your gratitude.

"What was my lesson here?"

"What did I need to change or learn?"

"How can I make this change in my mental and emotional processes?"

*Be sure to reality test what is true for you instead of
forming an automatic habitual response.*

*Celebrate these milestones by recognizing them and slowing
down to take a moment to feel into them.*

A LASTING HAPPINESS

Happiness is derived from:

- Worthiness of Life's Gifts
- Sense of Balance
- Connection to the Fabric of Life
- A Feeling of Wholeness

Meditation

Sit quietly, relax and take several deep breaths. Scan your body for any areas of tension and breathe into those areas and release the tension.

Reflect now on love, happiness, abundance, health and wellness. Move deeply within your heart. Take a deep breath and remove any tension within the heart. Here you will find the core of your true self. A place that is untouched by pain.

Feel your wholeness beneath the pain of unhappiness. Have faith that you have everything you need to experience true happiness and joy. Allow this faith to be your guiding light.

Now feel into your heart and breath in joy, allow your feelings of happiness to bring you peace. Stay with this experience and hold it close to you. Let it be a reminder that your life is beautiful and you are free to create your life's desires.

Now allow gratitude to fill your heart, bringing to you a release from disappointment and feel your spirit becoming free, making your life easier and lighter. Gratitude opens the door to our heart so it can receive more happiness in your life.

Feel the freedom and enjoy your happiness.

VII

❧❦

THE PRESENT MOMENT

LIVE IN THE PRESENT MOMENT

A lot of our pain, bitterness, anger, shame and guilt has to do with our memories—even if those memories are just yesterday or this morning. If our memory was erased, we would not have any of those emotions. We experience them because we are allowing something that we are remembering, consciously or subconsciously, to stimulate our thoughts and feelings. Without a past, there can be no pain, anger or guilt.

Anxiety and fear are the stuff of the mind about what might or might not happen in the future, even if the future is one hour from now. The present moment does not create such emotions, and there is no other reality than the present moment. We cannot go to the store to buy something yesterday, nor can we go now to buy something tomorrow.

We cannot act in the past or in the future. We can only act

in the present. Only in the present can we make decisions or respond to events or challenges. Only in the present can we exercise our free will to change our lives. The only point of power to create and change our lives is the present moment.

There was never a time that was not now. There is no other time.

Living in the Past and Future

One Cannot go the Store Today and Wish to Buy Something Yesterday or Tomorrow...

- Produces Anxiety and Fear
- Cannot be Present and Aware
- Power is found in the **Present Moment**

The Story

The Monks and the Lady of the Night

Two travelling monks reached a ford in a river where they met a young lady of the night. Wary of the current, she asked if they could carry her across. One of the monks hesitated, but the other quickly picked her up onto his shoulders.

Together the monks strode through the river until they reached the other side, and the monk set the woman down on the other bank. She thanked him and continued her journey.

As the monks continued on their way, one was brooding and preoccupied.

Unable to hold his silence, he spoke with anger. "Brother, our spiritual training teaches us to avoid any contact with women—let alone that sort of woman—but you picked that one up on your shoulders and carried her!"

"Brother," the second monk replied, "I set her down on the other side, while you are still carrying her."

EXPERIENCE

Each of our lives speaks a language of its own, one that no one else really knows. We must accept the truth of what is in the present moment, translate the mystery that has been written on our wall and transform all that we think through the knowing heart. Our experiences in life ask each of us to enter the humble process of self-discovery again and again, so the act of living life reveals and untangles both the questions and the answers.

Each life is a unique puzzle, like a mystery to be solved, and each of us is an alchemist. When we are thrust into our experiences in life, we often feel conflict within. It represents incongruences between what we think in the mind and what the heart knows. The mind has a thought, and this thought creates an emotion.

DIALOGUE

Christina Reeves:

If we want to experience the joyful divinity of every present moment, we will need to let go of the illusory feeling of separateness created by our senses. The truth is, we are spirit, energy and matter connected with the all that is. If we find ourselves living this lower energy self and feeling lost in the midst of pain and hurt, we must ask for guidance. The only expectation that we can truly have is when we exchange our feebleness for faith and we engage in prayer with the full bluntness of our emotions and pain. It is in this moment that we have the only absolute expectation knowing that all is well. We actively expect to be restored, and we don't need to know how, what or when. This is where we will find true and lasting Joy.

Dimitrios Spanos:

It is so true that our mind is guided by the past and keeps contemplating the future. Essentially our mind is on constant interpretation of the past and in survival mode towards the future. However, when we rise above our thoughts and emotions, we begin to realize that between the perception of the past and wonderful dreams of the future, lay the magnificence of the present. This is the most important moment of our life, one that resonates with our soul-spirit experienced in our body.

RECOGNIZING OUR PATTERNS

What am I Thinking?

Making It Personal

We will need to address our patterns to uncover the conflict and the struggle you may find yourself in as we speak. Here are some questions to assist you in the discovery process:

Where is my thinking from—past or future?

What emotion am I feeling with my thinking?

What do I believe or what fundamental understanding do I have about my thinking?

Did I choose this thinking, or was this something I was taught?

Do I value this thinking? If so why? If not, can I let it go?

EXERCISE

The moment we stray from the present moment, either to the past or to the future, we create a tension between two places: where we are and where we are thinking from. This splits our attention from the present moment, and this is where the choice points and clarity reside.

To uncover the conflict and the struggle you find yourself in, here are some questions to assist you in the discovery process:

Where is my thinking from—past or future?

_____

_____

_____

What emotion am I feeling with my thinking?

_____

_____

_____

What do I believe or what fundamental understanding do I have about my thinking?

_____

_____

_____

Did I choose this thinking, or was this something I was taught?

_____

_____

_____

Do I value this thinking? If so why? If not, can I let it go?

_____

_____

_____

How can I remain integral in my Awareness?

_____

_____

_____

What are some of the obstacles preventing me from staying in my present moment?

_____

_____

_____

How can I stay aligned in the present moment?

_____

_____

_____

How can I make a practice of living and knowing Oneness?

_____

_____

_____

EMBRACING NEW PERSPECTIVES

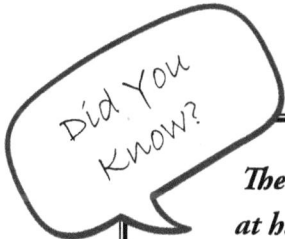

Did You Know?

The only moment there is or ever will be is always the moment at hand. Each present moment leads to the next moment and is most important to the sanctity that is within each experience. Each moment contains an internal and external perspective, which opens us to the flow of life that carries us all.

REFLECTION

The Present Moment cannot be anything other than this.
Wishing it were different cannot make it different. There are certain things you can do to make some moment in the future different than it might be. But the future is not now.

You will never find happiness in the future—for it is the all that is right now, with things exactly the way they are right now that creates our future.

If you love the way things are in this moment, or at least completely accept them the way they are, you will be happy. If you don't, you will suffer, wishing things were different.

ASK YOURSELF:

We are drawn to experiences that teach us what we need to know in very real ways, and the gift of the experience might be waiting on the threshold of your curiosity. The present moment is the most important moment of our life, one that resonates with our soul-spirit experienced in our body.

How important is freedom from the constantly thinking mind?

_____

_____

_____

Would you like your life to move like the flow of water currents on a smooth river along the rhythms of nature and beauty?

_____

_____

_____

Do you want to live life with passion? If your answer is yes to the above, then let life unfold within the present moment.

_____

_____

_____

How can I make a practice of living and knowing Oneness?

_____

_____

_____

HAVE FUN JOURNALING

Consider journaling an experience that touched you with such a great depth of emotion that you were not able to stay in the present moment. What was preventing you from doing so?

Write about an experience you had where you were able to remain calm in your present moment.

What was the experience asking of you beyond the pain and suffering?

What was contained within the experience of the present moment that helped you grow?

How might you develop and maintain integrity; advance consistency with what you think, feel, say, and do—in your present moment?

Take some time to ponder and process your experience of the present moment. Assess and reassess. If any actions are necessary, ask yourself what steps you can take to be proactive.

CONNECT WITH OTHERS

Start a conversation with a friend or loved one, sharing your experience and your insights from your journaling.

Now **tell a story** of a time where you paid too much attention to the mind stuff and were unable to remain in full Awareness to what was unfolding in your life in a present moment.

In retrospect, describe the missed opportunity to see a deeper meaning of the experience and to initiate change. By not living in the present moment, how might the experience have misled you or impacted you in a negative way?

Now, **perform active listening** and ask your friend or loved one if they would like to share their experience of a similar nature.

Milestones

We will all encounter endless life experiences. Our ceaseless
efforts to engage in living our life fully involves a commitment
to keep what is true while living in the present moment.

While remaining in our present moment, we are able to align ourselves
with the higher frequencies of the Life Force Energy in all things.

This is a never-ending practice of tuning our inner
self to the mysteries that surround us.

In doing so, it is important to celebrate the milestones of
honoring what we are experiencing, and by keeping only
what is real and visible in the present moment.

What milestones are you celebrating?

Living in the Present

The heart is beating and the lungs are breathing deeply. The light of our soul is visible.

- Experience joy, love, and appreciation
- We are engaged and grateful

Meditation

Close your eyes, sit quietly and relax. For a few moments, simply place your attention on your inhalation and exhalation. Feel yourself relaxing deeper now. Scan your body for any areas of tension and breathe deeply into any place that may be tense.

As you experience your body, hold the thought that you are a valuable human being, worthy of love and open to kindness. You are a light in this world, and you deserve affection and love.

Support yourself knowing your value by honoring your needs and treating yourself respectfully. Allow yourself to love your body, accept your emotions and pay attention to your thoughts in the present moment.

You do not need to be perfect in order to accept yourself, and there is nothing you need to do or achieve to have self-respect. You are worthy because you exist. Simply honor yourself and feel this goodness in your life.

Imagine now how your life would be if you accepted yourself and every moment of your life as the absolute perfection that it is.

Imagine if you stopped wishing any moment were different than it is right now. If you wished you were in a relationship or a different relationship, wished you had more money, success or fame, wished your health were better, wished you were enlightened, wished anything were different from the way it is right now... what would happen if instead you simply accepted the great gift of this moment exactly as it is?

Just imagine this for a moment and you will begin to see that the result of doing this will bring great happiness, satisfaction and fulfillment because it will be in alignment with truth and with reality.

The only difference between your happiness and your suffering is not the way things are in the moment, but rather your response to this moment. It's your acceptance or rejection of this moment and what is arising in this moment.

Now imagine how different and happier your life would be if you did this one simple thing. Simply accept what is happening in each moment exactly as it is without wishing it would change in any way. Each moment cannot be other than what it is. Wishing it were different does absolutely nothing but make you suffer. Embrace reality. It's really quite wonderful, no matter what it is or how it appears to be.

VIII

RIDING OUR EMOTIONS TO FREEDOM

GOING DEEPER

Emotions are one of the main things that derail communications and persuasions. Once people start getting upset at one another, rationalism goes out of the window. If you can identify and control your own emotions, you have a good chance of avoiding conflict. If you can sense the emotions of others, you have a better opportunity to resolve the issue. And, of course, it all starts with you and your own emotions.

The ability to balance emotion and reason in making decisions leads to good decisions and right action. Emotion should not be abandoned, lest cold and callous decisions are made. Nor should logic be abandoned unless you want a wishy-washy outcome.

Emotional literacy means being able to label emotions precisely. This includes the emotions of others, but especially your *own* emotions. It also means being able to talk about emotions without getting overly emotional or (as happens with many people) denying them. Emotional literacy is not using "I feel…" statements to offer opinions, ideas, etc. Thus, "I feel that is a good idea" is not emotional literacy, whilst "I feel angry" is. Being emotionally self-aware means knowing how you feel in real time.

The Story

The Boy and the Fence

Once there was a little boy who had a very bad temper. Every time the boy lost his temper, his father handed him a bag of nails and told him he must hammer a nail into the fence.

On day one, the boy realized he had hammered 37 nails into that fence. He really did have a bad temper!

In the days that followed after that realization, the boy gradually began to see his temper and set out to control it over the next few weeks. Each day, the number of nails he was hammering into the fence slowly decreased. He soon found out that it was easier to control his temper than to hammer those nails into the fence.

A day finally came when the boy didn't lose his temper at all. Upon hearing this good news, his father suggested that the boy should now pull out a nail for every day he was able to control his temper.

The days passed, and finally, the young boy told his father that all the nails were gone. The father took his son's hand and led him to the fence.

"You have done well, my boy, but what do you see about the fence?

The boy looked at the holes in the fence.

His father asked him, "Son, will the fence ever be the same?"

The boy shook his head no.

Yes, nodded his father, "When you say things in anger, they leave a scar just like these holes left in the fence. You can put a knife in a man and draw it out. It won't matter how many times you say I'm sorry; the wound is still there."

Moral of the story: control your anger, and don't say things to people in the heat of the moment that you may later regret. There are some things in life you are unable to take back.

EXPERIENCE

It is clear that on our evolutionary path, we have taken on the challenge of conscious evolution. It is also clear that we have been given the gift of the mind as the map to understanding the process to achieve this goal. The mind offers us the ability to pay witness to ourselves.

Self-knowledge is the first step in being able to handle emotions. If you can see them and name them, then you at least have a chance to do something about them. Empathy is the ability to feel and understand the emotions of others. If you can empathize, you can engender trust, as people desperately want to be understood at the emotional level.

Emotional Intelligence means taking primary responsibility for your own emotions and happiness. You cannot say that others "made" you feel the way you feel. Although they may be instrumental, the responsibility is yours. There is no such thing as "someone else made you do it."

We must learn to appreciate and accept differences between people, understanding that we have different priorities and capabilities around emotion.

EMOTIONAL DETACHMENT

Did You Know?

By not learning to name the emotions and discerning the correct emotional response, it leaves the person distant and emotionally detached from those around them.

DIALOGUE

We Are NOT Our Emotions

Christina Reeves:

The mind is the map, and by working with the mind, we can bring our old experiences to light for transformation. This is our test: the time is now, while temporarily encased in these physical bodies, we can remember our true nature and the course of the true nature of our parents, spouse, children, siblings, co-workers, friends and enemies. Whether we can remember the true nature of divine beings that have incarnated into other religions, nationalities, races, genders or political or philosophical ideologies, we have come with the challenge of breaking through the veil of our self-imposed ignorance and the emotions and life situations created by those illusions.

Dimitrios Spanos:

Yes, we are spiritual beings—all of us are embedded into the world of spirit. As its dynamic essence enlivens all creatures and creations and now more than ever, we need to believe that SPIRIT IS OVER MATTER, and the deeper we embrace spirit, the deeper we move into our higher nature. We have been given the free will and power to do this. We need to keep balancing our emotions, thoughts, feelings and thinking and transform them through the power of our will.

THE ROLE OF EMOTIONS

Emotions are a State of Mind

Emotions do no depend on outside circumstances.

Emotions are influenced by thoughts, and thoughts are influenced by our childhood programming and beliefs.

When We Choose the Inner Door to Darkness

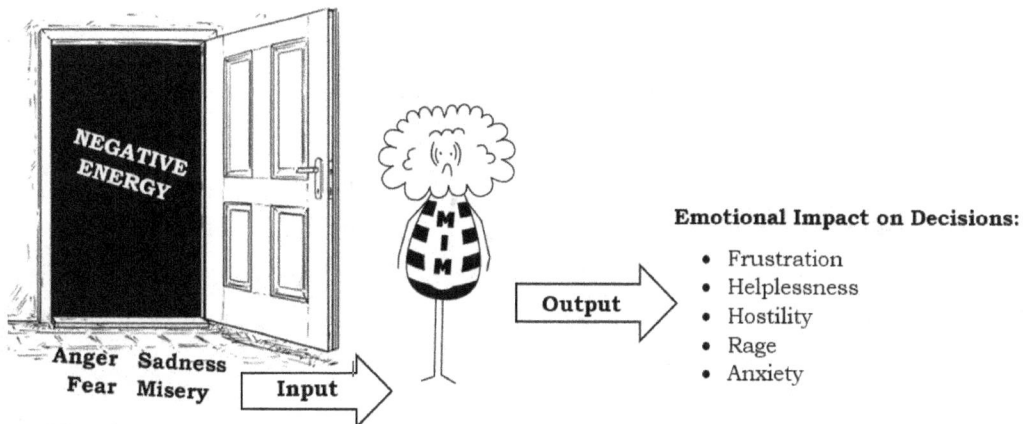

NEGATIVE ENERGY

Anger Sadness
Fear Misery   Input

Output

Emotional Impact on Decisions:

- Frustration
- Helplessness
- Hostility
- Rage
- Anxiety

OUR PATTERNS

Differentiating Our Emotions and Feelings

MAKING IT PERSONAL

At our present stage of evolution, emotions are a main source of our life energy and creative power. When properly used, they can guide us to the truth and to ever greater states of freedom and happiness.

Emotions are complex. Every day, our experiences affect them. Sunshine or rain clouds, our favorite song on the radio or an angry email at work—all of these can affect our mood, change the way we feel and influence the way we think.

The problems come when we allow those feelings to dictate how we deal with others. Why? Because emotions can cause us to react differently in a certain moment than we would normally. If we're feeling especially happy, we might agree to do something we wouldn't otherwise do. If we're feeling very down or upset, we might unintentionally take those feelings out on someone.

Everyone experiences primary and secondary emotions. If you're finding it hard to differentiate your feelings or you're feeling emotionally detached, then getting help doing so is essential to living a fully connected life. Living a life that isn't full of emotion or compromised emotional responses are disrupting that is unnecessary and often lonely.

Emotions are a disturbance, and the particularly positive ones seem to reside beyond the negative emotions on a much deeper level at the core of our true essence. When we speak about getting our emotions "under control," we are usually thinking about controlling our response to emotions. This isn't easy, but it can be done with practice. As we explore our entire range of emotions, we will be able to feel the un-disturbing positive emotions; the ones that do not cause us pain and suffering.

EXERCISE

We have all been blessed with the ability to take the experiences handed to us and seek the gifts within the experiences, thus transforming them into something extraordinary. This often requires a shift in our perception along with a knowing that both feelings of joy and despair come from within and have nothing to do with the actual experience itself; remembering that we are only seeing our own perception of the experience.

One incredibly useful skill is that of seeing the big picture. In essence, seeing the big picture involves the process of awareness, the stepping back in an emotionally charged moment, and thinking about the consequences of our actions—both short and long-term.

Here's how it works: If you receive an email that bothers you, step away before you reply. If a friend or family member does something frustrating, pause before you react.

Then, ask yourself questions like:

- How will my response affect my relationship with this person?

- Will I regret saying or doing this tomorrow? How about next week? Or next year?

This doesn't have to take much time. In fact, once you gain practice, it becomes more of a habit.

Our relationships are like bridges between us and everyone else. Every day, you're faced with moments that are charged with emotion. When you take a moment to see the big picture and adjust accordingly, you add another brick to strengthen and reinforce the bridge—instead of allowing those moments to slowly wear the bridge down, until it falls apart.

REFLECTION

Our feelings are useful emotional tools for us to understand our experiences and to understand ourselves. It is best to remain with the feelings, experiencing them fully until there is nothing left to feel.

Then comes the moment to move on to a deeper discovery process of reflection and shift the attitude we have regarding the experience. Allow this processing of the experience to occur, in fact, ask for it… ask to be shown the deeper meaning of the experience while remaining the observer of your thoughts and feelings.

Old wounds are caused by painful experiences that remain in our memories and return to play out when we get triggered. Wounds are formed in the context of relationships from an early age, and we tend to follow our learned habitual responses similar to our initial reactions to the old experiences. We keep carrying them in our mind as counterweights, and not only do they keep holding us down, but they also influence our decisions and behaviors in our present moments—often in conflicting ways.

Choose an experience that causes you an emotion that you would like to transform.

Reflect back on your life to your earliest memory you have of feeling this emotion.

See if you can discover the belief you had or the root cause underlying the emotion.

Reality check to see if this is truly what you believe or is it someone else's belief written on your wall.

ASK YOURSELF:

From a place of playfulness and genuine curiosity ask yourself the following:

What is it that is actually bothering me, triggering these emotions?

_____

_____

_____

What do I feel?

_____

_____

_____

What are the emotions that I feel at this moment?

_____

_____

_____

What do I believe (consciously or subconsciously) that is forcing me to feel these emotions?

_____

_____

_____

What may have happened in the past that may have programmed me to believe these beliefs, and what is now causing my pain or unhappiness?

_____

_____

_____

What is my lesson here?

_____

_____

_____

What do I need to change or learn?

_____

_____

_____

How can I make this change in my mental and emotional processes?

_____

_____

_____

HAVE FUN JOURNALING

Sometimes, we are deeply wounded by the very same people we love, as well as those who love us. Wounds that have not healed will remain within us, sitting right behind our thoughts and feelings until they are transformed. Healing comes when we stop defending our beliefs, hiding them or projecting them onto others.

We must be willing to feel things fully and ride all of our emotions to freedom, leading us to the alignment of our local self to our higher nature, higher intelligence and higher consciousness.

Begin a journal about your experience with an emotion you are dealing with that causes you pain or frustration.

Be prepared not to have either all the questions or answers, but instead simply remain open. Our tendency is to try to solve all the problems rather than allowing ourselves to have time to process and allow more questions to come up.

And again, as in previous chapters, although it may seem painful and not efficient even when we feel sure that we have the answer in our mind, it is often best to complete the journal entry with a question rather than an answer. This question will then work in the subconscious mind calling forth answers, intuition (tuition from within), inspiration and guidance from within.

CONNECT WITH OTHERS

Start a conversation with a friend or loved one, sharing your experience and your insights from your journaling.

Practice active listening while encouraging the other person to tell their story of where they are with their emotions.

Reflect with your friend or partner on both stories and discuss any missed opportunities for identifying and feeling their emotions fully and how needs, attachments or beliefs might have interfered with the outcome of their experience.

Milestones

Few of us have a very intimate contact with feeling our emotions. When someone asks, "What are you feeling?" we often answer vaguely, such as bad, unhappy, upset, disturbed or negative.

We want to get more specific when describing our emotional state by using words which accurately describe the emotion we feel. Each time you take a moment to feel into your emotions and name them accurately, you have reached another milestone.

Celebrate these milestones by recognizing them and slow down to take a moment to feel into what is true for us instead of simply answering with an automatic habitual response.

When We Choose the Inner Door to Light

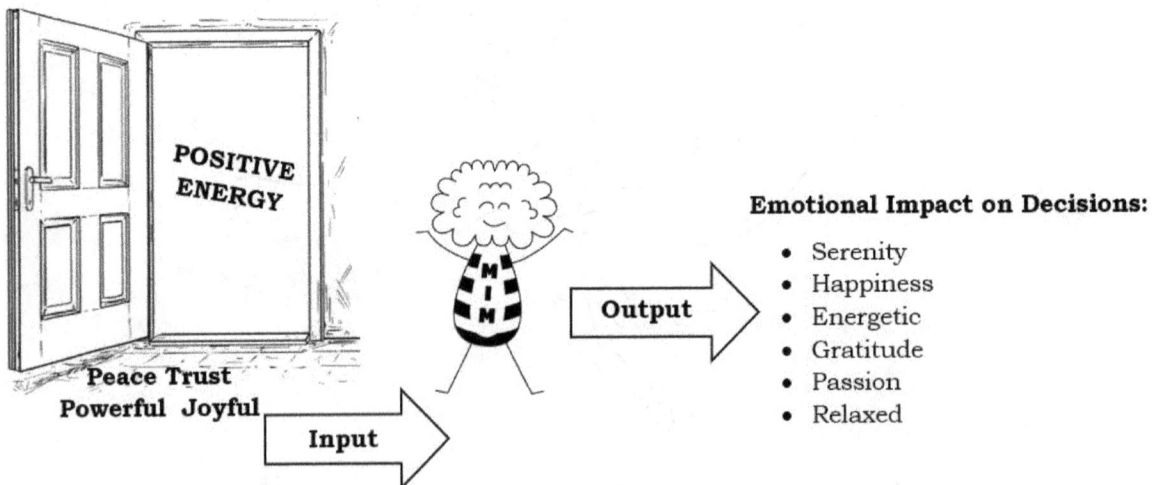

POSITIVE ENERGY

Peace Trust
Powerful Joyful

Input

Output

Emotional Impact on Decisions:

- Serenity
- Happiness
- Energetic
- Gratitude
- Passion
- Relaxed

Meditation

Sit comfortably. Relax and take several deep breaths. Feel your rib cage expand with each breath. Feel the power of your breath push open your chest cavity and feel your back expand filling your chest with air. Let go of the mind stuff. Release any negative emotions you may be holding in your mind or your body on your exhale. Keep breathing in light and love and breathing out all negativity.

When you are relaxed, feel your inner presence as if a quiet gentle power carefully guides you to your center of balance and calm. Connect to this inner power in a conscious way and feel at one with this power.

Integrate the responsibility of your power as you create a vision of a balanced and wholesome way of living in the world and being one with yourself and one with others. See yourself in this vision. Feel that this inner power is soft and quiet; feel it guiding you carefully, teaching wisdom and truths about yourself and how to engage with others. Notice that power need not be aggressive or forceful in order to succeed at its tasks. It is yours to use to express the love, grace and goodness of your being.

This time as you breathe in, say "YES" to yourself relaxing deeper as you exhale. Now breathe in saying "YES" to your life, relaxing deeper on the exhale. Again, breathe in saying "YES" to your spiritual forces, relaxing deeper on the exhale. Finally, breathe in again saying "YES" to your power.

Be willing to recognize the power of love within you and as a power that moves through you, feeling it as a unique expression of your divinity. This power is yours to carry out into the world and a clear definition of who you are. It brings healing to the world and allows you to be a beacon for good. Use your power to free yourself from negative emotions and use this power to create a wholesome and happy life.

IX

CREATING A SOLID FOUNDATION

"This being human is a guest house. Every morning is a new arrival. A joy, a depression, a meanness, some momentary awareness comes as an unexpected visitor... Welcome and entertain them all. Treat each guest honorably. The dark thought, the shame, the malice, meet them at the door laughing, and invite them in. Be grateful for whoever comes, because each has been sent as a guide from beyond." -Rumi

The strength of our spiritual foundation is ultimately revealed by how we live our lives, especially in terms of disappointment and challenge. We so often forget that we are living so close to the Earth and that it is alive. This vast Earth carried us our whole life, and yet we often are not paying attention to the thousands of ways it speaks to us, all without words. Yet, our need to build our relationship with what holds us up seems essential.

If you have a heart that is filled with hurt or a mind that is fogged over with despair, just as the seed buried in the earth cannot imagine itself as a flower, the mind and heart cannot image itself loved or at peace. The courage of the seed is to crack wide open and move from the dark into a blossom, and this is also the work of our soul.

We cannot escape the world; however, we must understand our part in it and move through it. We cannot avoid the tangle of living our lives as the world keeps interchanging us with the chaos of experience as it has its way with us. As much as our mind feels compelled to sort out all of our experiences and separate life with our preconceptions and preferences, there is nothing that will stand in the way of our direct experience with life.

The Universe will have its way with us. The simple and profound things that matter in life are repeatedly shown to us in our experiences as a way to bring our full attention to them, and it is best to lean into them, meeting them while standing upright in full awareness. The bliss and wonder are waiting for us, but we must accept the gift. The things that matter repeat themselves through our loving hearts, whereby the pain and fear of the experience fades and moves us into Wholeness once again.

Once we have anchored in a strong foundation for our lives based on our values and virtues, we are able to interface with the world from a place of empowerment and compassion. We must express the choices that define and honor us. What we like, desire and choose are reflections of our individual choices that help carry us through the emotional and spiritual initiations that make us strong, resilient and more conscious individuals, teaching us who we are at a foundational level. No one can diminish this foundation because it is the rock of self that illuminates our world.

The Story

Wise and Foolish Builders

This is parable about two men who each decided to build a house. The two men went out looking for the perfect place to build the house.

The first man was very wise. He thought carefully about the kind of house he wanted to build. He wanted a house that was strong. If a strong wind or heavy rains came, he did not want his house to break up or wash away. This wise man knew that the most important part of a house is the foundation. The foundation is the first thing that is built. It is the bottom of the house. The foundation has to be sturdy and strong to make the house sturdy and strong.

The wise man looked everywhere until he found the perfect place. He found a huge flat rock and knew the rock could be the foundation for the house. The wise man dug around and chipped the rock until it was the perfect size for his house, then he built his house on the rock.

After he was finished, he lived in the house. Many times, storms came to his house. The winds blew and the rains came, but the wise man sat comfortably in his house. He did not worry about the storms because he had built his house on a rock.

The other man that built a house was foolish. He did not think carefully about the kind of house he should build. He just found a nice flat place and started building. He built his house on sand. The foundation kept slipping and sliding in the sand, but the foolish man did not care. He just wanted to build a house.

When the foolish man finished his house, he moved in. When the first storm came, the winds blew and the rains came down and the foolish man's house fell apart. It fell apart because it did not have a strong foundation.

The Lesson of the Story: The house represents how we choose to live our life. The wise man was someone who had strong values and virtues—he lived with awareness and common sense, followed the laws of the universe and did not see a separation between himself and all that is. When a person builds his life in this way, he is building a strong foundation. He will be strong inside.

The foolish man in the parable was someone who lives unaware of his place in the world. He does not live in the awareness and connectedness of all that is, and because he has not built his life on values and virtues, he will not have a strong foundation. He will be weak inside.

> *"Life has no other discipline to impose, if we would but realize it, than to accept life unquestioningly. Everything we shut our eyes to, everything we run away from, everything we deny, denigrate, or despise, serves to defeat us in the end. What seems nasty, painful, evil, can become a source of beauty, joy, and strength, if faced with an open mind. Every moment is a golden one for those who have the vision to recognize it as such."* - Henry Miller

EXPERIENCE

We want to create a foundation that is as strong as the concrete foundations of a house that can hold our life in place. Without a strong foundation, the irregularities and mishaps of life will buffet us about and wreak havoc in our lives. Our Spirit will not survive well with constant change, and we will be like a feather in the wind.

We thrive well with consistency, and we function well with stability in our lives. When the foundation of our life is healthy, it expands and supports our life more fully. We can take on more responsibilities, be more creative and be more playful. A healthy foundation is flexible, yet at the same time enjoys the daily rhythms of life. This stability allows us to be more patient as our life unfolds: less reactive and less volatile to what is external to our being as we learn to accept life as it is. A strong foundation also helps us to maintain our spiritual connection when the winds of change blow in our lives.

When building a strong foundation in our lives, we can relinquish the need to defend our point of view, and we will feel no need to persuade others to accept our point of view. Instead, we have an inner knowing of right actions and good deeds. Within each of us lays the wisdom of our world, and in the wisdom lays the freedom and willingness to step into the field of all possibilities, a place where we can surrender ourselves to the creative mind that orchestrates the dance of the universe. The more we commit ourselves to building a strong foundation, the more secure we will feel. It is through this wisdom, we will find our security…. its strength lies within.

Security from Outside Sources:

- Materials
- Lifestyle
- Relationships with Others

DIALOGUE

Inner Security

Christina Reeves:

True and lasting security does not come from anything exterior to our being, rather it is inner security that regulates us and gives us a sense of well-being. It allows us to let down our guard, relax and recharge our Life Force Energy. True security is not found in the outer material world, nor is it found in our relationships with others. It is this inner security we need to cultivate, and it is our connection to our Divine Source. When we have this peace within, it releases us from fear and worry about our survival.

Dimitrios Spanos:

Indeed, dear friend, you have outlined the great benefits of living free from the old paradigm of security's superstition; we all must realize that there is no such thing as security. A long time ago, security existed only in Paradise. Now, living in today's world requires that we develop the willingness to let go of securities, break down the emotional prison walls and allow our heart's courage and determination to embrace all possibilities.

We must remember not to act like an oyster that closes to protect its pearl and let our soul shine. We keep searching for life's beauty and grace, keep moving ahead and choose to open the door to our destiny.

RECOGNIZING OUR PATTERNS

Embracing Our Personal Power

MAKING IT PERSONAL

Developing a strong foundation in our lives is another way we develop our personal power. It means being responsible for our actions and our choices. It is not about what we do to others or what is done to us, it is the development of our inner strength, knowing who we are, what we want and our willingness to be responsible for claiming that for ourselves. Our personal power comes from within. We empower ourselves by affirming our lives, knowing we have a place in the universe and we do make a difference. It is this empowerment that cements our foundation in place and enables us to be a force for good in the world.

BACK TO THE BASICS

Did You Know?

The important bricks to building a strong foundation are:
Patience, Security, Stability, Structure and Administration.

EXERCISE

Building a good, strong foundation that anchors our Life Force Energy in the physical plane ensures our survival and the quality of the life we live.

Patience is indicative of a strong and healthy foundation. If we are restless, constantly moving from place to place, job to job, or relationship to relationship, the foundation is both weak and undefined, and we will not have strong boundaries to hold the Life Force Energy. This will create restlessness and a constant desire for change. Patience is a defining quality of our foundation; it allows us to firmly and fully root ourselves into life. We can only be truly creative and happy when we are rooted in our own life.

We all want to feel secure in our lives, but what many of us perceive as security does not exist. True security is not found in the outer material world, nor is it found in our relationships with others. In fact, true and lasting security does not come from anything exterior to our being. It is inner security that regulates us and gives us a sense of well-being. It is an absolute knowing that we are a part of the whole that allows us to let down our guard, relax and recharge our Life Force Energy. It is inner security we need to cultivate, and it is our connection to our Divine Source. When we have this peace within, it releases us from fear and worry about our survival. Ultimately, it helps us create reserves of Life Force Energy for going through challenging times. We need only experience this inner security in order to feel protected in all aspects of life.

Inner security lets us thrive, and in doing so, we come to know the truth and beauty of our spirit. Inner security helps us to remain focused on the good in our lives and lets us define healthy boundaries that provide a margin for comfort, ease and assurance.

Stability keeps us steady through change. It implies being balanced and having the ability to be flexible and move with the flow of life. It stops us from becoming reactive or feeling threatened. Stability allows us to focus on our inner world. It supports our awareness and gives us a clear perception of the world around us. When we are stable, we know what is best for us and how to readjust ourselves to remain steady and constant. Stability helps us to trust in life.

Structure permits us to create rhythm and routines which define our daily activity. It supports us in maintaining a foundation that will hold our gifts and talents so they can develop. Structure gives strength and purpose to our efforts. Structure is power.

Administration is the ability to organize and manage our lives so we have a sense of control of the external factors that influence us. It suggests order in how we use our time, energy and resources for the highest good. We will want to eliminate waste and dissipation because they interfere with the flow of life. Those who have given up on their dreams have difficulty manifesting what they need for their survival and often fall into despair. Others who administer their lives carefully and realistically have a strong, healthy foundation and experience abundant vitality and joy in simply being.

REFLECTION

Life itself holds the mirror of our experiences in front of us to reflect our choices; may we see the reflection of spiritual knowledge in our consciousness that encourages freedom and asks us to be as one with all that exists in our world. We can develop and strengthen the foundation of our lives, and this begins within ourselves. We can become champions of unconditional love and freedom from oppression of all varieties, and we can be a source of healing to the planet and all those around us.

Through the curious and wondrous process of self-discovery, we often stumble beautifully into the spaces between our thoughts and our suffering. Living in Awareness challenges us to see everything from a higher perspective, discovering the truth that holds us all, daring us to mix the elements of the world through our hearts and minds making all things visible. All of us are here to help unravel each other and to make our way back to love through the mirror of life.

Take some time to reflect upon the foundation of your life.

Reflect on an area in your life you are challenged with.

Now, take a moment to reflect on your comfort level.

ASK YOURSELF:

What does your living presence say to you about your current foundation?

_____

_____

_____

How can you move closer to building a stronger foundation?

_____

_____

_____

How comfortable are you with feeling into and internalizing your experiences related to building a stronger foundation?

_____

_____

_____

Are you able to let go of your internal argument with your experiences or with life?

_____

_____

_____

Can you trust the underlying wholeness of life that waits beneath your internal arguments?

_____

_____

_____

HAVE FUN JOURNALING

From a place of Awareness instead of reacting, give yourself a moment to evaluate your visions of what a strong foundation feels like.

Observe yourself and your current foundation.

See if you can see the bigger issue.

Notice the triggers, and take action using words of compassion to de-escalate the emotions and the angst of the experience.

This step is to Choose Your Highest Self.

Listening to your heart, I invite you to journal about a question you are currently carrying related to the foundation you have created.

Call to this question honestly so it might open a door in your life right now.

Now, from a place of Awareness, see yourself below the illusion in the wonderful gritty nature of things as they are by listening, translating, and questioning your experience.

Which part of you opened the door to a new realization?

Was it your active listener—your deep inner knowing—or your seeker of the truth?

CONNECT WITH OTHERS

Now go ahead and if possible, connect with the others in the experience. Remember what's truly important to you. Have consideration of the others and move forward with those in mind.

Start a conversation with a friend or loved one, sharing the experience and your insights from your journaling.

Tell the story of your experience, not from a victim's point of view, but by way of an example of that small part of your life.

Share how your experience opened up a larger sense of life simply by giving it your attention.

Discuss your experience and what insights or questions surfaced for you.

Hold a loving space for yourself and the others as you find your way to building a stronger foundation in your life.

You can use these four questions:

What am I feeling?

What options do I have?

What do I really want?

What action steps do I need to take?

Milestones

When we listen with our heart, we allow the reality of things to touch us beneath the surface of our identity. When we are authentic and real, we come closer to what matters, and the questioning and listening draws us away from our familiar habitual logic into the realm of perspective, a view of reality and eternity.

Celebrate the milestones of courage it takes to sit still with patience in the not knowing or the courage to say what you see in your discovery process through your own inner vision.

This is how the soul opens the door so we can begin to make sense of our experiences in life. Realize that we are never separate and that while we live in the Universe, the Universe is also always within us. Spirit lives everywhere, and we are one in spirit. Our spiritual body detects the workings of Spirit, and we all have within us an inner living light of primordial, ever-present, non-dual Awareness that lights up our whole of creation.

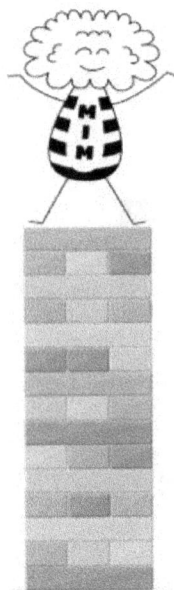

Security from Inner Sources:

- Knowledge of our Inner Beauty and Strength
- Stability
- Awareness
- Courage of the Heart

Meditation

Sit quietly and relax, breathing into the base of your spine. Scan your body for any areas of tension you may be holding in your energy. Now breathe into any place that feels tight, congested or sore.

Feel the strong arms of Spirit holding you steady and firmly in your foundation. You cannot fall or fail in life; the spirit of you watches over you and protects you against all harm, and in the arms of spirit you are always safe and stable.

Feel this strength and grace in your spine, in the core of your belly, down your legs and in your feet. This strength comes from calling Spirit to you. Know that Spirit will always guide you to higher ground. You may not know or understand your life path, but you will know you are safe and protected as you journey through life. Invite Spirit into your life, and ask Spirit to stand with you. It feels like a great rock that shields you and protects you; supporting you as you are standing upright, living in truth and in your integrity. Spirit is always a resource you can call on. Feel yourself carried in the arms of Spirit and you will begin to trust its presence in your life.

Ask for guidance by saying, "Beloved Spirit, one who has known me through lifetimes, thank you for your love and protection. I appreciate your vigilance and constancy in watching over my soul. You have given me encouragement when life seemed unmanageable, and celebrated my accomplishments. Thank you for showing me the way and to know my values and virtues as the living force within me. I know how deeply you love me. Show me how to deepen my trust in myself and in life and to surrender to the higher good."

X

LEARNING TO LIVE LIGHTLY

"We need to find the 'middle way' in our own lives. It is the art of finding balance. Reflecting upon our lives, we soon discover what serves us well—nurturing calmness, ease, and simplicity. We also discover what it is that leads to entanglement, confusion, distress, and anxiety. Wisdom is being able to discern the difference, then knowing what we need to nurture and what we need to learn to let go." - Christina Feldman

To Live Lightly is to live a life in balance, neither pushing or pulling at the Life Force Energy. When living lightly, we understand that our Divinity is only dependent on arriving at perfect inner peace. We can achieve this peace through realizing the ultimate truth and unconditional love, and we manifest truth and love when we are free of the mind's control.

There are a few attributes to living lightly, and they are:

Being healthy requires a willingness to move and live the life of the body, bringing to us vitality and resilience that comes from our Life Force Energy. Learning to love the body just the way it is is the gift of a healthy and loving mind and heart. Building in pleasure, giving the body time for rest and regeneration is essential for Living Lightly.

Our ability to love ourselves, forgive the past and honor our needs defines the level quality and depth of feeling found in unconditional love. It is through unconditional love for ourselves that we bring in the Life Force Energy and the forces of healing into our lives. We love ourselves without reserve or doubt, we honor our needs, feel our feelings and express our truth is a measure of how well we love ourselves. Unconditional love puts an end to sacrifice and the need to prove our worth, and it frees us to Live Lightly.

Ease and pleasure fuel our well-being and bring us joy. Both are essential components for Living Lightly. They are the ways we relax, let our hair down and have fun. Spiritual maturity requires a balance between being able to work hard and play well, accepting the complexities of hardship and ease, frivolity and gravity. Real ease involves doing what you like, when you like. Some people who work and toil too hard dry up and lose their edge, while others indulge themselves too much, not wanting to take on any responsibilities. Living Lightly requires finding the middle ground; the balance of self-love and discipline.

Prosperity reflects a belief in your innate worth to be loved, blessed and fully supported by a loving, caring Universe. Allowing prosperity to come into your life reflects a belief that you are worthy of receiving your good and you acknowledge it as a right when you claim it for yourself. Abundance reflects your right to pleasure and joy while living your best life.

The Story

Over-identification is Misery

A Sufi was going through the marketplace of the town with his
disciples. He was a very observant man. He would use everything
he saw with his eyes or heard with his ears for teaching, as
he understood there was a lesson in every experience.

He witnessed a man who had a rope round a cow's neck and was dragging
the cow through the street. The Sufi said to his disciples, "Stop this man,
and surround him and the cow, I'm going to teach you something."

The man stopped when he heard this, for the Sufi was a famous mystic. He
wanted to listen to the lesson and wondered what it had to do with him
and his cow. The Sufi said to his disciples, "Let me ask you: who is bound to
whom? Is this man bound to the cow, or is the cow bound to this man?"

"It's obvious," the disciples said, "this man is the master. He is holding
the rope, and the cow has to follow him wherever he goes. The cow is
bound to the man. He is the master, and the cow is the slave."

The Sufi took out his scissors, cut the rope, and the cow escaped. The
man was running after the cow, and the Sufi said, "Now look what
is happening! Now you will truly see who is the master; the cow is
not interested at all in this man—in fact, she is escaping."

The man was very angry, he said to the Sufi, "What kind of experiment is this?"
The Sufi turned to his disciples and said, "And this is so with your mind."

Moral of the Story: all the nonsense that you are carrying inside is not interested in you. You are
interested in it. You are holding onto to it somehow, and you are becoming mad in keeping it
together. But you are interested *in* it. The moment you lose interest, and the moment you understand the futility of it, it will start disappearing; like the cow, it will escape.

EXPERIENCE

Living a life in balance is Living Lightly; knowing that "The Kingdom of Heaven is Within." We cannot read, hear, watch or think our way to the experience of it. However powerfully evocative they are, these will only bring us to the frontiers of our personal process of discovery.

We cannot come to the experience by reading a description, however profound and articulate, or looking at photos, however beautiful.

Living Lightly is only experienced when all that appears ceases, including the experiencer-perceiver. We will need to remember and remind ourselves, re-concluding, again and again, the concept, that "All there is, is Consciousness." It is here that we will know the experience of dissolution and bliss of Living Lightly that comes when the mind has been liberated and the heart has been illuminated from within.

LIBERATION OF THE MIND

Did You Know?

"All there is, is Consciousness." It is here that we will have the experience of dissolution and bliss that comes when the mind has been liberated and the heart has been illuminated from within.

DIALOGUE

Power vs. Force

Christina Reeves:

Power does not mean trying to force an outcome in any experience. Power arises from meaning; it has to do with motive and principle, and it is always associated with that which supports the significance of life itself. Power is noble, it appears to that which uplifts, dignifies and ennobles. Power requires no justification and is associated with the whole. Power is still; it is like a standing field that doesn't move. Power doesn't move against anything at all… it remains still. Power is total and complete within itself and requires nothing from the outside; it makes no demands and it has no needs. Power energizes, gives forth, supplies and supports. Power gives life and energy.

Dimitrios Spanos:

Christina, you are absolutely right, power has nothing to do with control. Most of us don't realize the power of the universe within us. Our Self embodies the union of opposites of our two natures (a higher and a lower) on both the personal and spiritual scale. We can discover our power by staying within the tension of our two natures. Power is still; it is like a standing field that doesn't move. Your experience of power as stillness creates powerful images, such as St. Michael, one of the strongest forces on Earth and Universe or the powerful stillness in St. Francis' prayer, which is a source of strength for all of us.

RECOGNIZING OUR PATTERNS

Why do I Isolate Myself?

MAKING IT PERSONAL

A big part of Living Lightly is the continuance to evolve to a greater sense of Awareness—to continue to grow ourselves, holding a loving space for others and for society as a whole as we evolve together as One.

Sometimes if we become absorbed in such efforts, we might naturally also become attached to our specific ideas of success, and when we do not, or until we do achieve what we consider our success, we might feel some frustration often resulting in rejecting ourselves, others and society. We might feel inferior because we have not yet succeeded or we feel whatever we are doing is not making a difference.

Becoming attached to any result, inner or outer, for ourselves or others, is a major source of anxiety, tension and conflict within ourselves and with others. While we do need to make an effort, we also need to learn to accept ourselves and others at each stage of our growth exactly as we are, as well as accepting our life situation as it is until we are able to change it.

Sometimes we may feel we have stopped growing. We're not interested in improving ourselves and, thus, we may become complacent about how life, society or the world is showing up from our perspective. There is a tendency towards isolation and to shut out the outer and inner worlds preferring to remain living the way we always have been, even if this is unpleasant and painful. Some people prefer a world that has become familiar rather than subject themselves to change and embrace the unknown, even though the unknown may hold the promise of greater happiness, peace and love.

EXERCISE

When we are Living Lightly, we are connected to a "higher love" that is present in the Universal Life Force Energy. This love is not the ordinary love of this world; this love is the center of all life. The heart is the center, the sacred chamber of love, and the temple of the Divine presence within us. It is the truth of our being and the conduit for love to flow through us. It never forgets an act of kindness or a moment of love and stores the memories of love deep within its hidden chambers.

In the process of personal growth, we need to make an effort towards transformation and accept that the Divine design of evolution will not allow us to simply rest. We can ignore it for periods of time, but sooner or later the life events and situations happening around us will force us to awaken, and we will need to accept change and transformation to emerge like a butterfly from its cocoon.

Living Lightly requires accepting and loving all aspects of one's self and of creation. We become the witness to all that is happening within and without and remember that all is divine. May we be curious and amused by the fantasies and fears of the mind, with no need to act upon them, if we realize that they will bring harm to us or others. May we simply be the watcher, accepting all, loving all and allowing all to pass into the nothingness from which it came.

Living Lightly empowers and encourages us to cultivate a belief in ease and to trust a higher spiritual wisdom for the experiences we have. It also helps to assist us in being clear about our choices for love. Spiritual consciousness is dependent on us accessing Unconditional Love. Once we have anchored and integrated it, we interface with the world from a place of empowerment and compassion. We are Living Lightly!

REFLECTION

Everything that exists is pure energy, and change and evolution is the stuff our entire Universe is made of. Staying with what matters involves setting down our opinions and preconceptions of how we would like things to be, and living directly into life as it is. Our work here is one of discovery processes, and one of trusting our intuition. It is the work of learning to live your inborn nature as it relates to everything, and to know you are a beautiful spark of life in all of Divine creation.

Our past experiences are the most helpful tools for learning about yourself. You are able to see how certain choices, behaviors and circumstances have led you to where the life you are currently living. You might even realize that the most effective way to improve your life was often counter-intuitive—against conventional wisdom and what you have been taught.

To enter the unknown (and sometimes even the unspeakable threshold of change) requires a soft courage and patience, waiting until the urging voices of our mind have nothing more to shout about; until there is nothing more to reach for and nothing left to let go of.

Love recognizes itself only in love. By choosing this Divine love and opening our hearts, it becomes the way of Living Lightly. It will keep our spirit strong. As we create the intention to claim this love, it becomes easier to allow it into our being—to embrace the wonder of love and to become aware of the times we feel separate from the source of love. At those moments, we must accept and allow life to bring us new experiences of the miracles of love in our ordinary daily life.

ASK YOURSELF:

In what ways are you Living Lightly? In what ways are you not?

_____

_____

_____

Are you accepting all areas of your life right now?

_____

_____

_____

What areas of your life do you wish to change?

_____

_____

_____

Are you resisting any aspects of your life right now?

_____

_____

_____

Are you allowing an injury, wound, or any perceived limitation to hold you back from living fully in life?

_____

_____

_____

Who is the one within you that says yes, and who is the one within you that says no?

_____

_____

_____

Listen to the mind chatter and try to hear all that is said (and even what is unsaid). What might you be pretending not to hear or know?

_____

_____

_____

Can you open to the soft moment in your center?

_____

_____

_____

Can you endure the wonder of uncertainty until it shows you another deeper way to live your life?

_____

_____

_____

What old way of living life can you let go of that will return you to the freshness of living lightly?

_____

_____

_____

HAVE FUN JOURNALING

Journaling helps us with the work of being and keeping things real. I invite you to write in your journal each day. Re-read and update it often as your discovery process moves you along to new insights.

By personalizing your conversation within your writings, you can explore even deeper as this becomes the living connection of all that is within you and all that holds the history of the presence and wisdom of your Highest Self.

Let go of trying to control the mind in your journal. One way to do that is to write with your non-dominant hand. While it may appear a bit messy, you will be surprised at what comes forth when we drop the urge to control.

Write a journal entry about any areas of your life where you don't feel you are Living Lightly. These could be areas that are causing you to lose your sense of balance or connection to others or your feelings of peace and wellbeing.

Be sure to include what you might believe that is causing any disturbances towards your ability to feel peace and wellbeing.

Try to capture all the emotions that come up for you when you think about cultivating peace and well-being in your life.

CONNECT WITH OTHERS

Living Lightly increases the flow of our Life Force Energy as we free ourselves from emotional pain and forgive hurt, allowing the universal energy of love to flow as the mighty river it is. We can feel the flow of universal love and simply allow ourselves to be fulfilled, no matter how that is expressed.

Start a conversation with a friend or loved one, sharing the experience and your insights from your journaling. Start by feeling into what's real for you and opening a discussion of the current state of your being with regards to Living Lightly.

Discuss ways to expand your self-worth, enhance your self-respect and honor the Soul within. What action steps might you take to develop a greater sense of self-esteem that enables you to Live Lightly?

Be sure to express the choices that define you and honor your personality as the individual manifestation of your light. What you like, desire and choose are reflections of your individual choices that help carry you through the emotional and spiritual initiations that make you a strong, resilient and more conscious individual.

It is important to remember that whatever is within your experience is never about the other person or anything external to us.

Discuss the current state of your heart and how it functions.

Does it function from pain, fear, worry, anxiety or does it function from love, peace, and unity?

Which comes naturally?

Which is most challenging?

Now considering how your heart functions, in what ways would you like to grow?

Milestones

Seldom, if ever, do we reflect back on the successes or milestones we have accomplished. Take a moment now to think about those accomplishments. Think about personal limits you had to deal or come to terms with. As you do this, you will begin to understand your patterns on a deeper level and this reflection will expand your perspective, having greater empathy for yourself and others than when you first recorded the events.

You may even find yourself examining issues which might have prevented you from fulfilling your potential. You will begin to get clarity about your role in life in the bigger scheme of things and work to change your beliefs and replace your old thoughts with more effective, empowering ones.

Take note of all the times in your life you have opened your heart until what you could not see or hear was received and felt internally and thoroughly enough to initiate change, altering the way in which you live in the world.

Reflect on all the times you were able to accept your experiences and were able to sit in stillness with enough patience and silence to allow this change to happen.

Record and celebrate these milestones along your journey. Each one of them reveals the path ahead and each one contains a promise of Living Lightly.

Meditation

Close your eyes and take several deep breaths. Scan your body for any areas of tension and release this tension by breathing into those areas. As you relax deeper, feel the flow of energy in your body.

Fill any remaining tense areas of your body with pink light. Breathe in the pink light and release the tension on the exhalation. Notice the ease and the release of tension with each breath. I invite you to let go, ease down and relax even deeper now. Feel the unconditional love, pleasure and healing power of this pink light as it fills your energy field and radiates out of your body. This energy feels good and it is comforting; as you relax and ease down into your body, you will begin to feel at home in yourself. Now forgive the past, release any hurts and let yourself go deeper.

As you continue to breathe in pink light, fill your energy field with the warmth of your own love. Feel your lower back relax and ease down as you release any pressure you feel to perform or be more than you are. Know that you are enough. Affirm that you are a child of God, worthy of love, prosperity, good health and happiness.

Ask for support in letting go of old thoughts that may haunt you with beliefs of unworthiness and self-loathing. Ask for help in knowing your wholeness or to acceptance of yourself as you are. Ask for help creating more balance, deeper acceptance and abiding self-love.

Feel your sense of oneness with life. Ask yourself where and who is your community. Who are the people you resonate with? Where are the people who share your ideas and who support you in being and doing your best? Think of the greater human community of which you are a part.

Envision happiness, fulfillment and oneness for all people in your community. Feel blessed as you consciously create a sense of oneness with them. We are the people, on planet and part of an expanding network of consciousness capable of doing great good. Allow your spirit to shine in all places where people come together for a greater good. Bless them for their individual efforts and collective manifestation on behalf of the whole.

"I affirm that I am a part of the family of man; I am never alone, and there is no separation. I bless all others in the spirit on oneness."

XI

LIVING LIFE WITH PASSION

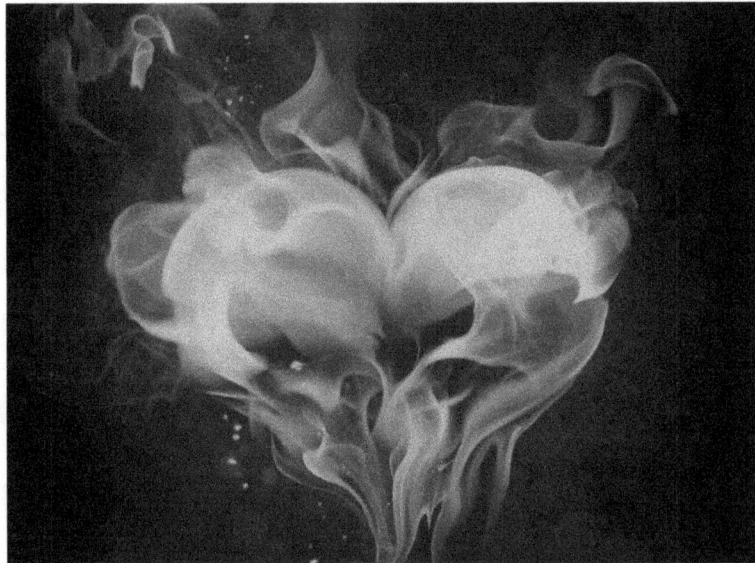

"When you are inspired by some great purpose, some extraordinary project, all your thoughts break their bonds; Your mind transcends limitations, your consciousness expands in every direction, and you find yourself in a new, great and wonderful world. Dormant forces, faculties and talents become alive, and you discover yourself to be a greater person by far than you ever dreamed yourself to be." -Patanjali

When you wake up, are you excited to start your day?

Do you wake up with a sense of purpose?

Do you have a Vision that makes you feel Energized?

For many of us, this is not the case, yet something inside of us knows that it is possible. You might feel like you are going to do great things, but you just haven't been able to figure it out yet or live it consistently. It begins with a goal. So, what is a goal really?

Well, the goal is what you can choose. A lot of people get hung up on the "Well, what is my purpose? You know, my destiny?" question, as if there is only one thing and they've got to figure it out ASAP. That kind of thinking holds up a lot of people because they don't want to start on a goal unless they think it is the right one. The real goal is more about saying than thinking.

What do you really want your goal to be? What are you really passionate about? How can you move down that road and how can you create this goal for yourself?

For the most part, we have not been taught to follow our passions. Although some people certainly have, and that's awesome, we're really not taught this idea. We are taught to follow a responsible route. To go to school, study, graduate with this or that degree, and then to go out in the world and get this kind of job or that kind of work and to work hard for many years and then you get to play.

Does this sound like you? "Well, I really want to do this, but I can't. I'd like to do this but what if…"

Sometimes we work for years covering our own wounds of esteem and the ups and downs of our accomplishments until our heart is covered over with only our perceived achievements. It is only when we lay aside our achievements that the light from our heart begins to take on a new form.

The light will never force itself into our hearts. It is very patient and seems to wait for us to open enough so the light can enter—filling whatever space we have been able to empty out within ourselves.

The Story

Passion is Everything

> The story is told that a dispassionate young man approached
> the Greek philosopher Socrates and casually stated, "O
> great Socrates, I come to you for knowledge."
>
> The philosopher took the young man down to the sea, waded in with him,
> and then dunked him under the water for thirty seconds. When he let
> the young man up for air, Socrates asked him to repeat what he wanted.
>
> "Knowledge, only O great one," he sputtered. Socrates put him
> under the water again, only that this time it was a little longer. After
> repeated dunking and responses, the philosopher asked, "What do
> you want?" The young man finally gasped, "Air; I want air!"
>
> "Good," answered Socrates. "Now, when you want knowledge
> as much as you wanted air, you shall have it."

The Moral of the Story: Whatever we can dream about already exists in the vastness of the sea of knowledge. If you want anything badly enough, you can find the willpower to achieve it. The only way to have that kind of desire and willpower is to develop passion. For you to achieve anything in life, passion must come first. Call it passion, commitment or conviction. Whatever the name, cultivate it in large measure. Sharing it constantly keeps it alive. Passion is not directionless; it is sharply focused around what we want to achieve. It is concentrated and, like a laser beam, cuts through objections, obstacles and negativity. It is hard to say no to living a life of passion when we care so strongly about something, and even more difficult to resist as we are drawn into our vision and become engaged. Whenever anything fires our soul, impossibilities vanish… this is the power of passion.

EXPERIENCE

You are a **CREATOR**. Creating our dreams embodies all of our longings and desires. They hold the promise of love through our spiritual connection as possibilities to be fulfilled. It is important to realize that we are co-creators with our source of all that is, and therefore, there is nothing we cannot create in our life. By allowing our dreams the time and space to unfold, we gain clarity about what we want and give them the opportunity to manifest.

In any area of life, especially when it comes to mind, perception, power, empathy, and so on, there is always a status quo. It's the place where a person says, "Well, that's enough. I'll settle for what I have. I'll stop here."

Sooner or later, this leads to boredom, frustration, problems and conflict. It ultimately leads to decline.

Imagination, which knows no such bounds, is the source for the most adventurous explorations. It can have a great impact on the material world, of course, but one mustn't conclude it is composed of matter or energy.

Imagination is non-material. To think otherwise winds you up in using some form of physics to depict imagination, and then you are imposing limits on it. This is an error. Imagination doesn't obey any laws of physics.

If imagination is the sincerest form of flattery, we've flattered reality enough. It doesn't need any more. Imagination creates new realities.

You can create the same thing over and over and eventually you'll be about as alive as a table. Inject imagination into the mix, and suddenly everything changes. You can steer that boat anywhere you want to. You can build worlds.

The lowest common denominator of consensus implies an absence of imagination. Everyone agrees, everyone is bored and everyone is obedient. On the opposite end of the spectrum, there are massive floods of unique individual creation, and then that sought-after thing called abundance is as natural as the sun rising in the morning. Sitting around in a cosmic bus station waiting for reality is what reality is. Everything else is imagination.

Then there are those who behave as though life is a museum. You walk through the rooms, find one painting, stroll into it and take up permanent residence. But the museum is endless. If you were a painter, you'd never decide to live inside one of your canvasses forever. You'd keep on painting. The relentless and obsessive search for all those things on which we can agree is a confession of bankruptcy.

When we re-learn to live through and by imagination, we enter and invent new space and time. But space and time aren't superior forces. They come into being when we turn on the tap of imagination. With imagination, one can solve a problem. More importantly, one can skip ahead of the problem and render it null and void.

Imagination isn't a system. It might invent systems, but it is non-material. It's a capacity. It feels no compulsion to imitate reality. It makes realities. Its scope is limited only by a person's imagining of how far imagination can go. The human race is obsessed with the question, "What exists?" It appears to be a far easier question than, "What do you want to imagine?" This comparison explains why civilizations decline. Imagination is a path. If you walk on the path long enough, you find the answers to all the questions you've ever asked. You find the power that people dream of.

DIALOGUE

Live Life with Passion

Christina Reeves:

Living a life of passion is learning to live love from the heart, adding new meaning to our lives. It creates a life that makes the heart sing with joy. As we create our dreams, we must be sure to follow the dreams of our heart and invoke the power of love that moves us even beyond the power of reason into a world of wonder and imagination. Living our best life is always living a life of passion, in one form or another.

Dimitrios Spanos:

Our world is blessed with so much natural beauty and has inherited much knowledge and great history. We have created amazing cities and towns, full of landmark buildings, monuments and masterpieces. We live with delightful traditions and customs full of magnificent beauty. All of these open up the interiority of our heart and allow us to experience tremendous appreciation for all that has given by God, ancestors, parents, life, family, friends and loved ones. Let us express our passion in a form of divine dance… lift our eyes upwards, open and raise both of our arms, fill our heart with appreciation and return our thankfulness to our creator-God.

RECOGNIZING OUR PATTERNS

Am I Living Passionately?

MAKING IT PERSONAL

When we are living our life on purpose and showing up for life with great passion, we joyfully create our life experience and become a valuable contributor to the experiences of others. We are not perfect—we forget and make mistakes—but when we remember our true self, we can re-assert this intention, and the fruits of our intention are revealed to us. This is bliss; this is passion!

There is almost nothing better in the world than the feeling of showing up for your own life. When we show up for life, we are actively participating in being a happy person, achieving our goals and generally living the life our soul really wants. Sometimes we may even feel that the energy of our future self is calling us towards our inspirations.

Look at your patterns of showing up for life. We cannot distance ourselves from life's inconsistencies, irritations and upheavals, but we can relinquish our desire for perfect order and gain peace of mind in the process.

In what ways are you not showing up for a life filled with passion?

In what ways are you not living a balanced life?

What changes can you make to balance work and passion?

What roles, if any, do you play? i.e., not good enough, victim of circumstance, "I can't do it."

Pay attention to the inner voice, what does it say about your passion in life?

Are you able to feel a strong desire to promote what you believe in?

What motivates you? What gets your juices flowing and raises your LLife Force Energy?

Become a passionate builder, a co-creator in sync with nature's rhythms, and ride the waves of energy. You will soon begin to feel more in harmony with life and the world around you. At times you will experience moments when you followed your bliss or passion and life flows easily; whatever is consuming your thoughts or that enthralls you is waiting for you to do something with it. The more that you become passionately fervent about things that speak so strongly to you, the more that you will notice that you can actually use this zeal to affect positive change in your life.

The Ultimate Pathway to Consciousness

Did You Know?

Imagination is the quality that outdoes reality: any kind of reality. Imagination is the infinite road. Consciousness wants to create new consciousness, and it can. Imagination is how it does it. If there were some ultimate state of consciousness, imagination would always be able to play another card and take it further.

EXERCISE

One of the ways to discover the limits of the life we want is to listen to our heart and use our imagination. Once you have written down your best life story, it is time to visualize your life, making sure to place yourself in the vision.

From the place of Awareness, become the observer of yourself as you walk around in your vision. Notice what you are doing in your vision from the heart, not the mind. Notice how it feels to you.

Now venture a little way past the vision into the energy of outrageous, awesome possibilities. Relax in this space, asking the following questions:

Is my vision the highest and best use of my life?

_____

_____

_____

Will this give me energy or deplete my energy?

_____

_____

_____

How do I define success?

_____

_____

_____

What am I grateful for?

_____

_____

_____

What are my blind spots?

_____

_____

_____

What am I pretending not to know?

_____

_____

_____

What good is there that I presently cannot see?

_____

_____

_____

How can I become the space for attracting this vision of my life?

_____

_____

_____

Stay loose and relaxed as you're conjuring up the various possibilities and be sure to take them all through the heart. You'll notice that some of them leave you with a feeling of intrigue, curiosity and feeling a bit lighter. These are your preferences. Now, let them tiptoe into your consciousness.

Simply allow them, watching them as an observer, to let the vision take form, leaving a vague impression, and then go for a bit more specificity as if you were bringing a camera into zoom focus. Allow and watch. If you remain playful and patient, the preferences forming in your consciousness will eventually become clear enough to describe the preference in more detail in your journal.

Still wait—don't jump the gun. Hold on a bit longer, and you will observe what I call maximum specificity by pinpointing the desires. Let them simply unfold. Stay with the vision. Take it to your heart and ask yourself, "What would be even better?" After allowing another answer to come into focus, ask yourself, "What would be even better than that?"

Repeat this process until you have an image of a life that is so perfect, you can't imagine any way to top it. This is pinpoint clarity. Once you have pinpoint clarity, practice visualizing your dream daily. I have found it is best to do this exercise first thing in the morning or last thing at night.

REFLECTION

Our lives are made up of a complex network of pathways that we can use to move from one phase of life to the next. For some of us, our pathways are wide, smooth and clearly marked. Many people, however, find that they have a difficult time figuring out where they need to go next. Determining which "next step" will land you on the most direct route to happiness, fulfillment and the realization of your life purpose may not seem easy.

Here are some attributes to reflect upon related to living a life of passion:

Positive Intentionality is focus and clarity of mind, heart and body to claim a desired outcome. It draws to us that which we long for. It is a major component for manifesting our dreams into reality. It works to align our feelings and desires with our hopes for our highest good and greatest joy. Intention lets us consciously claim that which we want is manifesting with each positive thought. We can back up our dream life with an absolute knowing, having faith that it will manifest and feel the love and gratitude.

Faith lives in our hearts to remind us that faith can move mountains. It is the essential ingredient for our hopes and dreams to manifest. Faith tells us we have the power to claim our good now. Faith sees us through our challenges and reminds us that we are all Divine children, capable of co-creating our best life. Faith gives us the courage to carry us through the deserts and out of the shadows into living our best life. Having faith in our Creator to see us through challenges, have faith in ourselves and in life itself. Faith is the guiding light.

Gratitude fills our heart with a sense of plenty and abundance. This releases us from disappointment and sets our spirit free. It helps us to appreciate and honor life, recognizing that there is good in all things and helps us to see all experiences as a blessing. Gratitude makes our life easier and helps us to live lighter, easing the spirit of heavy burdens. This allows our spirit to soar in appreciation for all the good in our lives. When we are grateful, we affirm "who" we are, and we affirm life itself. Gratitude is a leaping off point for manifestation; it opens the doors of our heart so we can receive more goodness in our lives.

ASK YOURSELF:

There are many ways to discover what the next step on your life path should be. If you are someone who seeks to satisfy your soul, it is vital that you make this inquiry. Often, your inner voice will counsel you that it's time for a change, and it is very important to trust yourself because only you know what is best for you.

To live a life of passion from the heart, ask some powerful questions:

What am I taking for granted?

_____

_____

_____

How can I show my appreciation for others?

_____

_____

_____

What can I do to take care of those I love?

_____

_____

_____

How can I be more present?

_____

_____

_____

Who am I blaming or mad at?

_____

_____

_____

Who do I need to forgive?

_____

_____

_____

Where can I be more accountable and what am I responsible for?

_____

_____

_____

What am I thankful for?

_____

_____

_____

How can I take better care of myself?

_____

_____

_____

What action do I need to take to make sure I have no regrets?

_____

_____

_____

HAVE FUN JOURNALING

Partner with the Universe. The Universe is made of pure energy—impersonal, unformed and intelligent. This means that we are free to create whatever we desire while accepting the energetic consequences of our actions. Because of this, there is no need for us to judge anyone. Our trust in the Universe means that we know each person is on their own path, learning from their own choices.

Our human mind wants to classify things to understand them, and since we live in a world of duality, we see good or bad, right or wrong. In fact, sometimes we cannot fully comprehend something without knowing its opposite. But you can transcend your mind to connect to spirit today, enabling you to feel gratitude for your own partnership with the universe and the path you follow without judgment.

For this journal entry, write in detail about the life you would like to live. People who get what they want tend to be the ones who make the effort to know what they want. If you feel confined in a tiny, limited life, imagine the life you would like to be living.

CONNECT WITH OTHERS

Sometimes we tend to protect our seeds of dreams, desires and passions by wrapping them in the business of our daily ambitions and grandiose plans that have nothing at all to do with the sweetness and ripeness that already exists within us.

Remember the story of the peach; none of our plans and goals can prepare us for the moment we ripen. What we can do is try not to define ourselves by all the layers covering us. When we are ripe within, our soul fills out like a mature fruit and once ripened, we are able to feel compassion and joy underneath the soft, fuzzy covering of the stories we got used to telling ourselves. Nothing matters but the sweetness within the heart.

Start a conversation with a friend or loved one, sharing the experience and your insights from your journaling.

Realize what is real for you and open a discussion of the current state of your being with regards to living life from your heart.

Discuss the current state of your life and how you feel about it.

Reflect on how many goals and dreams you have incubated and all the hours you have spent weaving your dreams into stories you tell yourself, some that never came to the fruition you hoped for.

Milestones

While celebrations are sometimes intended to honor life's more momentous occasions, much of real life tends to happen during the in-between times. While moving from one moment in time to the next is seldom considered a significant occurrence, it is during those in-between times that we are most in tune with life's most profound, albeit simple joys. Celebrating the in-between times can be as easy as paying special attention to them when they do happen, rather than taking them for granted.

The beauty of Life is happening all around us and to us between the pauses that we take to honor our journey through life. It's our focus of attention that can turn an in-between time into a celebration.

Pay homage to each moment by slowing down and allowing yourself time to look around at the beauty of nature by opening your heart and mind to take in all of life's wonders. Far too often, we let those simple moments of awe pass us by. Celebrate this major milestone to begin to live a life of passion from the heart.

Meditation

Sit quietly, relax and take several deep breaths. Scan your body for any areas of tension and breathe into those areas and release the tension.

Reflect now on love, happiness, abundance, health and wellness. These are all aspects of God bequeathed to us by the Divine as part of our spiritual heritage. Understanding and claiming this truth is how our dreams come into fulfillment when we back up our dreams with absolute faith that they will manifest.

Begin this meditation by reflecting on something you truly want in your life right now. Hold the image of what you desire as if it had already manifested. Use all of your senses to feel this vision and claim it for yourself now. Experience it in your body, feel it in your heart, see it in your inner eye. Know that it is real. Our thoughts create our reality. The more you imbue your dream with your feeling senses, the stronger the vision becomes.

Now move deeply within your heart. Take a deep breath and remove any tension within the heart. Here you will find the core of your faith. Have faith in your Creator to assist you, have faith in the Spirit to bless your life. Have faith that you are never alone and you can meet all the challenges and initiations you may face. Allow faith to be your guiding light.

Feel into your heart and breathe in joy, allowing your vision to bring you joy. Stay with this experience and hold it close to you. Let it be a reminder that your life is beautiful and you are free to create your life's desires.

Now allow gratitude to fill your heart with a sense of knowing your dreams will come to fruition. Gratitude brings a release from disappointment and sets our spirit free, making our life easier and lighter. Gratitude opens the door to our heart so it can receive more.

XII

CREATING OUR NEW STORY

"Never lose an opportunity of seeing anything that is beautiful, for beauty is God's handwriting— a wayside sacrament. Welcome it in every fair face, in every fair sky, in every flower, and thank God for it as a cup of blessing." -Ralph Waldo Emerson

Walking the path of Spirit requires that we cultivate a highly-refined Life Force Energy field within us and around us; a field that carries the spiritual dimensions of our life within it. It also requires a highly-refined state of mindfulness. As we develop internal awareness, we can be assured that we can become and act as a radiant beacon of light for ourselves and our world.

The deepest wounds of separation are healed at this level of consciousness, reminding us that nothing about our character, our relationships and our life is written in stone. We can create new realities for ourselves—realities that serve us better, that are easier and make us happier. This can occur by directing and creating circumstances that bring us to the awareness of truth, love and healing. How we implement all these attributes and qualities in our lives and relationships is always our choice. We can make it fun and creative, or serious or challenging, but the task of reconciliation is ours alone to do.

Creating our dreams embodies all of our longings and desires. They hold the promise of love through our spiritual connect as possibilities to be fulfilled. It is important to realize that we are co-creators with our source of all that is, and therefore there is nothing we cannot create in our life.

Positive Intentionality is focus and clarity of mind, working to align our feelings and desires with our hopes for our highest good and greatest joy. Intention lets us consciously claim that which we want is manifesting with each positive thought. Back up your dream life with an absolute knowing, having faith that they will manifest and feel the love and gratitude.

Faith lives in our hearts to remind us that faith can move mountains. It is the essential ingredient for our hopes and dreams to manifest. Faith sees us through our challenges and reminds us that we are all Divine children, capable of co-creating our best life. Faith gives us the courage to carry us through the deserts and out of the shadows into living our best life. Faith is the guiding light.

Gratitude fills our heart with a sense of plenty and abundance. This releases us from disappointment; it sets our spirit free. It helps us to appreciate and honor life recognizing that there is good in all things and helps us to see all experiences as a blessing. Gratitude makes our life easier and helps us to live lighter, easing the spirit of heavy burdens. When we are grateful, we affirm "who" we are, and we affirm life itself.

Forgiveness releases our heart from the burdens of negativity. Sometimes we might want to place ourselves on a negativity diet. Listen to and watch empowering programs and news, and try to stay away from anything or anyone that causes us to feel stressful. Forgiveness is currency for the soul; without it, we would accumulate so many negative experiences we would crumble under the weight we carry. Our heart would be heavy with anger, negativity and stubbornness. We forgive for the sake of love. It sets the spirit free and opens the heart once again to love freely, and allows our Life Force Energy once again to resume its natural flow.

The Story

Triple Filter – Socrates

In ancient Greece, Socrates was reputed to hold knowledge in high esteem.

One day, an acquaintance met the great philosopher and said, "Do you know what I just heard about your friend?"

"Hold on a minute," Socrates replied. "Before telling me anything I'd like you to pass a little test. It's called the Triple Filter Test."

"Triple filter?"

"That's right," Socrates continued. "Before you talk to me about my friend, it might be a good idea to take a moment and filter what you're going to say. That's why I call it the triple filter test.

*The first filter is **Truth**. Have you made absolutely sure that what you are about to tell me is true?"*

"No," the man said, "actually I just heard about it and…"

*"All right," said Socrates. "So, you don't really know if it's true or not. Now let's try the second filter, the filter of **Goodness**. Is what you are about to tell me about my friend something good?"*

"No, on the contrary…"

*"So," Socrates continued, "you want to tell me something bad about him, but you're not certain it's true. You may still pass the test though, because there's one filter left: the filter of **usefulness**. Is what you want to tell me about my friend going to be useful to me?"*

"No, not really…"

"Well," concluded Socrates, "if what you want to tell me is neither true nor good nor even useful, why tell it to me at all?"

NOTE: This is why Socrates was a great philosopher and is held in such high esteem.

EXPERIENCE

There are aspects of the Divine presence living within us that carry the power of reconciliation, healing and grace for our lives. When we awaken and are living the path of spirit, we can see how we have been guided through many circumstances (and many people) to take the next step on our path with a spiritual consciousness of our life, and the circumstances and choices others made as well.

At this point, we are open to receive direct guidance from the higher realms and the mystery of life unfolds before us as we follow a path of light, wonder and mystery. Living our life in this way, we are building and containing all the Life Force Energy we need to live a conscious, happy and intentional life; a life whereby we understand that it is sustained by our indelible link to the Source of all that exists. It is the link to spirit through our prayers, petitions, visions and hopes at the level that we know all that we need is provided for us and that we are blessed in endless ways that fulfill our best life.

The qualities of living the path of Spirit with Divine presence are: Bliss, Beauty and Serenity.

Bliss is the highest state of spiritual consciousness we can achieve and still remain in our body. It is the blessing of the Christ Light and the Holy Spirit, and it creates the space within us where we live in the grace of God. In this space, we know at the heart of all things, that all is well regardless of how they seem to appear. We no longer become hooked into the dramas and enmeshments that create frustration and anger. We fully accept life as a miracle. This state is often called enlightenment, as we have a direct experience of who we are. It is a perfect state of peace, acceptance and compassion. We have no craving, anger, desire or fear in this state… that is the stuff of the external and has replaced by the experience of complete oneness with all of life. Bliss is the inner space where we are untouched by the mundane and still carry out our daily tasks. We live our lives in the moment and respond with love rather than reactivity when we are challenged. As we begin to acknowledge and live the higher purpose our lives, we begin to walk the path of destiny. In this state, we cultivate love, compassion and truth and we are not only co-creating our best life, but we are doing so in a reality of wholeness.

Beauty is intrinsic to our being; it is the shining light of our soul emanating through us into the world around us. It is a quality that comes from God when we live our deepest connection with life, meaning we are beautiful regardless of what the external manifestation appears to be. It couples the warmth of spirit with the qualities of love, peace and serenity. Beauty is a reflection of our soul… simply a clear reflection of who we are. It is never a well-made, cold object, but is something that is permeated with spirit. It is an experience of grace manifesting in form. It contains within it a feeling, a vision or an object made with love and potential in our abilities to create and the potential of all around us. To the ancients, beauty was considered to be a virtue enabling people to forget, momentarily, their mundane existence and see the higher good and reflection of God. Beauty is a metaphor for the inner truth of our being.

Serenity brings delight and happiness in our lives. This is a state of quietness that combines the joy of harmony and the peace of tranquility. It is an inner place that reflects our highest truths, deep abiding love for the self and compassion and love for others. It implies absolute acceptance of what is. It has a fragrance of its own that is a rare perfume that calms our senses and assuages our appetites. Serenity is a spiritual quality and a goal worth cultivating in the disquiet of our busy lives. It holds the world steady and keeps our tasks proportional to our capabilities when creating our best life. It is never reactive or overbearing; it is a state of mind that soothes, heals and sustains. Choosing a path of serenity as a lifestyle requires a willingness to embrace the highest truth that everything is in perfect order and God is working in everything, even the chaos we see in the world. It is possible to remain in a serene state when we reflect on the Divine presence and know we are carried in love by the great spiritual forces of creation. We need simply to ease down and relax in self-acceptance and non-judgment. It is a way of saying yes to life, yes to the moment, and yes to how it feels; saying yes with gratitude and love.

DIALOGUE

Expression Of Beauty

Christina Reeves:

Beauty is a reflection of our soul… simply a clear reflection of who we are. It is never a well-made, cold object, but is something that is permeated with spirit. It is an experience of grace manifesting in form. It contains within it a feeling, a vision or an object made with love and potential in our abilities to create and the potential of all around us. To the ancients, beauty was considered to be a virtue enabling people to forget, momentarily, their mundane existence and see the higher good and reflection of God.

Dimitrios Spanos:

Our soul is nurtured by beauty. What food is to the body, uplifting, pleasing sublimating images are to the soul. The search for our beloved requires understanding and experiencing of Beauty. For our soul, beauty is the quality, the depth that invites contemplation and opens our heart to the whole world of divinity and agape. Our soul's desire is to engage in the subtlety and lightness of images that create unconditional love. Our soul longs for depth in beauty that invites contemplation and opens our heart to a whole world of divinity. What I mean by contemplation is the highest expression of beauty's depth and the invisible and beyond aesthetic beauty of the surface; the beauty that I see without seeing and the beauty that I know without knowing. The kind of beauty that dwells from the seat of my heart that I experience after I touch the hand of God and the beauty that connects me to Universal light, energy and love.

RECOGNIZING OUR PATTERNS

Overcoming our Limits

MAKING IT PERSONAL

We make an individual choice to invoke and affirm the power of the Holy Spirit working in our life, and as we evolve into mature spiritual beings, may we experience how God illuminates and transposes our lives to higher ground with each challenge we face, each act of love we offer and each moment of which we are aware.

We transform any limiting understanding of reality into an expanded awareness of how spirit works within each of us and make our world richer and our life happier. We need only look deeply into the truth of our being, know our thoughts, strengths and weaknesses and our purpose so we can indeed create the life we desire. We need only move through what is dank and old and unloving in our consciousness and become aligned to the nature of compassion, love and healing, transforming what has been perhaps previously outside of the realms of reconciliation to live the path of Spirit.

As we unite our consciousness with God, we embody the Christ Light allowing this light to strengthen our body, affirm our worth and honor our choices for creating our best life. In choosing this light, we honor the light in everyone we meet and enhance the collective light of all humanity radiating into the world.

Kindness is our loving Spirit in action... The greatest joy the Spirit knows is to share its light and love with others. Unlike the ego, which is driven by the question, "What's in it for me?" Spirit feels complete and wants to share its satisfaction with as many as possible. To share our spirit with another is one of the most healing and empowering experiences we can create.

Kindness is the act of our Divine nature to take over and lead our lives. When we are kind, we embody this nature and use it to feed and fuel the light in our world. To be kind is to live with grace, dignity and elegance. It means taking an interest in life and caring about it enough to make it better for us and for others. It's a powerful and profoundly self-loving choice because the kinder we are to others, the more love and kindness will return to us.

Kindness is a choice to honor the Divine in all, including ourselves. This action from awareness takes practice until it becomes a habit and we have the will and discipline within us to develop the habit of kindness, easing the harshness of life and feeding our Spirit.

A basic aspect of kindness to self is to create and honor healthy boundaries and to be clear and direct in communicating them to others. Many of us were taught that we have no right to personal boundaries and that saying no or respecting our own needs is selfish. Fortunately, that old school of thought and programming of self-sacrifice is starting to dissipate, and we are now learning to be clear to ask for what we need without hesitation or guilt. When we live with healthy boundaries and we feel free to express them, we create the opportunity to connect with people honestly, without confusion or manipulation. Everyone feels safer and more grounded.

Learn to live love from the heart, and it will add new meaning to our lives; a life that makes the heart sing with joy. As we create our new story, be sure to follow the dreams of our heart and invoke the power of love that moves us even beyond the power of reason into a world of wonder and imagination. Living our best life is always living love in one form or another.

No matter what the Universe sends, it has to be accepted as a gift and a loan from God. This means we must keep embracing all kinds of events and keep revealing life's magic knowing that each time you face opposition, you are getting closer to your destiny.

You become consistent in practicing processes, such as embracing the precious present moment, being aware of habitual patterns and old beliefs, and living within the tapestry of life.

Remain open to the idea that, although we live in an unpredictable world, each day there are new meaningful coincidences and situations and each and every one of these will shape your life and create your new empowering story.

EXERCISE

Another aspect of kindness to self and others is simply placing ourselves (and managing our lives and our affairs) in a realistic timetable. This makes room so there is no rush, and we can relax into life leaving the stress and entering the Spirit of grace. This is love in action. It is the accelerant for our soul's desire to grow and expand our peace. Slow down, relax and allow quality rather than quantity to be our highest goal in life. Kindness sometimes means "doing" less, and it means allowing mistakes. Kindness allows time and patience. It allows encouragement and forgiveness. It allows us all to pursue our life path without shame and fear. It allows the dignity of Spirit to lead us in life. Know that simple kindness begets kindness and ripples into the world like the waves in the ocean. Allowing ourselves more kindness and affording more of it to others is the one self-loving expression of Spirit that keeps on giving.

We need to consciously release and let go of all that is unlike love. Through gracious love, we are able to let go of suffering and hardship and find our way back to living mindfully from of the heart. We must be willing to let go of the past; divest ourselves of worries and burdens and allow love into our hearts. This one action will bring in the joys of love again and the ability to express it fully.

The collective Humanity needs each of us to build our individual spiritual bank accounts, and as we learn to merge the individual will with that of the Universal will, the ego will have been diminished, the accounts balanced and strong, and we will experience true freedom.

The important thing to remind ourselves of is that we need to spend this wealth (love) to all those around us and further within our communities and out into our world so we can all live in peace and freedom; so that we can all live open, loving and joyful lives. We do this through acts of kindness, understanding, compassion and love.

Life is soft, simple and easy, and each of us has something special to contribute to the whole. May we all become wealthy and may we all spend our love freely and wisely.

REFLECTION

Focus on Some Attributes for Cultivating Kindness to Self

Self-worth is a primary quality. It is a measure of how much we love and value ourselves. The more we value ourselves, the less dependent we are on the world to define us. We create our own identity rather than the world giving us an identity. Sometimes it takes many years to develop; as we go through our unique experiences and challenges, we are learning that we are always worthy of love, kindness and respect. This truth releases us from having to prove ourselves to others and makes us intolerant of anything that diminishes our value. When we connect to self and identify with our sacred nature, we love and accept ourselves exactly as we are.

Self-respect defines the boundaries of what is acceptable and what is not. It protects our wholeness, our dignity and our value and keeps what is noble shining brightly like gold, preventing our spirit from becoming tarnished. Self-Respect lets us say no when boundaries are crossed and forms a natural protection that filters out unkindness and bad behavior from others. In this way, we protect our precious selfhood.

Self-esteem affirms the hard work and levels of accomplishment we have achieved in our life. It is present in our life when we do our best and are proud of our efforts. This can also mean being responsible for a family member or standing up for what we know is right. It is what we are most proud of, not what the world defines for us. Self-esteem builds character and defines the way in which we value our actions and efforts. It honors the light within us as we continue to live our best life.

Self-confidence comes to us when we know we can do something well. It might be that we have moved beyond our fears and doubts to a level where we can manage our lives and meet our challenges head-on. When we have self-confidence, we develop greater levels of power, allowing our natural sense of worth to shine. It develops our willingness to address the challenges we meet with a certainty we can.

Empowerment comes from knowing our strengths, living our truth and always choosing to be free and unrestricted in our personal expression. Developing this personal power means being responsible for our actions and our choices. It is not about what we do to others or what is done to us, but it is the development of our inner strength, knowing who we are, what we want and our willingness to be responsible for claiming that for ourselves. Our personal power comes from within. We empower ourselves by affirming our lives, knowing we have a place in the universe and we do make a difference. Empowerment enables us to be a force for good in the world.

Freedom of Choice is the acknowledgement of our self-worth, self-esteem, levels of confidence and empowerment. This Freedom is about our ability to choose our good, and in freedom, we choose the best life for ourselves. We fill our best life with love, beauty, health, prosperity, unity, peace and joy. As we mature in spirituality, we value freedom as one of the greatest gifts of life. Integrating freedom is how we claim our God-given gifts and talents and how we express our being in the world. Living in freedom takes choice to the highest level of personal expression.

Life itself holds the mirror of our experiences in front of us to reflect our choices; may we see the reflection of spiritual knowledge in our consciousness that encourages freedom and asks us to stop being slaves to external ideas or situations. We can develop and strengthen these attributes within ourselves and become champions of freedom from oppression of all varieties, becoming a source of healing to the planet and all those around us.

There is a "higher love" that is our Life Force Energy, and this love is not the ordinary love of this world. This love is the center of our lives; the heart is the center of our Life Force Energy. It radiates from our heart which is the sacred chamber of love, and the temple of the Divine presence within us.

ASK YOURSELF:

What are the benefits of the following aspects in relationship to creating my New Story? What can I do to achieve these attributes?

Health is vitality and resilience and comes from our Life Force Energy. Health means we have regenerative ability and can create reserves of this energy for times of challenge.

Am I willing to move and live the life of the body?

_____

_____

_____

Do I love my body, just exactly as it is, accepting the gift of a healthy and loving mind and heart?

_____

_____

_____

Do I give my body time for rest and regeneration?

_____

_____

_____

Unconditional Love: As a measurement of how well we love ourselves, we might ask the following questions:

Am I able to love myself without reserve or doubt?

_____

_____

_____

_____

In what ways do I honor my needs, feel my feelings and express my truth?

_____

_____

_____

_____

Am I able to practice forgiveness and release the grip of negativity that I sometimes allow to have power over me?

_____

_____

_____

_____

Am I able to love unconditionally and put an end to sacrifice and a need to prove my worth?

_____

_____

_____

_____

Ease and Pleasure fuel our wellbeing and bring us joy. Both are essential components for a healthy physical life. Consider the following questions as you process this:

What are some of the ways I relax, let my hair down and have fun?

_____

_____

_____

_____

In what ways do I reward myself for hard work and responsibility?

_____

_____

_____

_____

In what ways am I able to balance between working hard and playing well?

_____

_____

_____

_____

In what ways am I accepting the complexities of hardship and ease?

_____

_____

_____

_____

In what ways do I find the middle ground; the balance of self-love and discipline?

_____

_____

_____

_____

Prosperity and Abundance reflect a belief in our innate worth to be loved, blessed and fully supported. Consider the following questions:

In what ways do I allow prosperity to come into my life?

_____

_____

_____

_____

In what ways do I feel worthy of what I say I want in my life?

_____

_____

_____

_____

Destiny is a Process

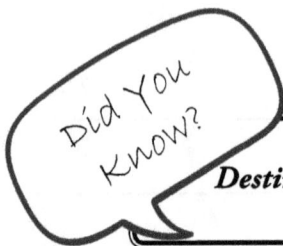

Did You Know?

Destiny is not something we create, but something that we work on.

HAVE FUN JOURNALING

We must express the choices that define us and honor our personality as the individual manifestation of our being. What we like, desire and choose are reflections of our individual choices that help carry us through the emotional and spiritual initiations that make us strong, resilient and more conscious individuals; teaching us who we are at a foundational level. No one can diminish this foundation because it is the rock of self that illuminates our world.

Using the information and insights you have gleaned from this workbook, take this time to write a letter to yourself. Write your new story; a story of your own creation. Keep it fluid and flexible—no needs, no attachments to any particular outcome. Allow the Universe to show you your true self by becoming an alchemist of your own heart and to reveal to you the purity of your soul, your highest self, the I AM of you and all that exists.

CONNECT WITH OTHERS

Start a conversation with a friend or loved one sharing your experience and your insights from your journaling.

Now, **tell a story** of a time where you paid too little attention to creating your life and simply allowed life to pull you this way or that way, or a time when you simply felt stuck in life and you did not feel happy.

In retrospect, describe the missed opportunity to see a deeper meaning of the experience and to initiate change, and by using your willpower, how might the experience have misled you or impacted you in a negative way.

Now **practice active listening** and ask your friend or loved one if they would like to share their experience of a similar nature.

Milestones

We will all encounter endless life experiences. Our ceaseless efforts to engage in creating the story of our life and living our life fully involves a commitment to keep what is true while reflecting, reinventing and creating the life we wish to live. This is how we are able to align ourselves with the higher frequencies of living our best lives. This is a never-ending practice of tuning our inner self to the mysteries that surround us and choosing those that bring us happiness and joy.

In doing so, it is important to celebrate the milestones of honoring what we are experiencing, and by keeping only what is working for us and building on this strong foundation to create something even better than that. We are always changing and always evolving to higher levels of consciousness.

Looking back on your life, and all the challenges that initiated big changes in your life, what milestones are you celebrating?

Meditation

Close your eyes and take several deep breaths. Scan your body for any areas of tension and release this tension by breathing into those areas. As you relax deeper, feel the flow of energy in your body.

Fill any remaining tense areas of your body with pink light. Breathe in the pink light and release the tension on the exhalation. Notice the ease and the release of tension with each breath. I invite you to let go, ease down and relax even deeper now. Feel the unconditional love, pleasure and healing power of this pink light as it fills your energy field and radiates out of your body. This energy feels good and it is comforting; as you relax and ease down into your body, you will begin to feel at home in yourself. Now forgive the past, release any hurts and let yourself go deeper.

As you continue to breathe in pink light, fill your energy field with the warmth of your own love. Feel your lower back relax and ease down as you release any pressure you feel to perform, or be more than you are. Know that you are enough. Affirm that you are a child of God, worthy of love, prosperity, good health and happiness.

Ask for support in letting go of old thoughts that may haunt you with beliefs of unworthiness and self-loathing. Ask for help in knowing your wholeness or to acceptance of yourself as you are. Ask for help creating more balance, deeper acceptance and abiding self-love.

Feel your sense of oneness with life. Ask yourself where and who is your community? Who are the people you resonate with? Where are the people who share your ideas and who support you in being and doing your best? Think of the greater human community of which you are a part.

Envision happiness, fulfillment and oneness for all people in your community. Feel blessed as you consciously create a sense of oneness with them. We are the people, on planet and part of an expanding network of consciousness capable of doing great good. Allow your spirit to shine in all places where people come together for a greater good. Bless them for their individual efforts and collective manifestation on behalf of the whole.

List of Needs

I — BE ACCEPTED
- Approved of
- Permitted
- Cool
- Be Included
- Be Popular
- Be Allowed
- Be Invited
- Be Tolerated
- Be Respected

II — TO ACCOMPLISH
- To Achieve
- To Reach
- To Hold Back
- To Fulfill
- To Profit
- Consummate
- To Gain
- To Attain
- To Win

III — BE LOVED
- Be Liked
- Be Special
- Be Wanted
- Be Cherished
- Be Desired
- Be Adored
- Be Esteemed
- Be Preferred
- Be Touched

IV — BE ACKNOWLEDGED
- Feel Good
- Be Worthy
- Be Flattered
- Be Appreciated
- Be Praised
- Be Complimented
- Be Valued
- Be Honored
- Be prized
- Be Thanked

V — BE RIGHT
- Have it My Way
- To Be Correct
- Morally Right
- Be Supported
- Not Mistaken
- Be Deferred to
- Be Encouraged
- Be Honest
- Be Confirmed
- Be Understood

VI — BE CARED FOR
- Be Embraced
- To Get Attention
- Be Saved
- Tenderness
- Be Helped
- Be Attended
- To Get Gifts
- Be Cared About
- Be Treasured

VII — TO BE CERTAIN
- To Be Clear
- Obviousness
- Commitments
- Accuracy
- Guarantees
- Exactness
- Assurance
- Promises
- Precision
- Sameness

VIII — TO BE COMFORTABLE
- Luxury
- Prosperity
- To Not Work
- Opulence
- Indulgence
- Taken Care of
- Excess
- Abundance
- To Be Served
- To Be Pampered

IX — TO COMMUNICATE
- Be Heard
- Make a Point
- To Be Listened to
- To Gossip
- To Share
- To Talk
- Tell Stories
- Comment
- Be Informed
- To Inform

X — TO CONTROL
- To Dictate to
- To Manage
- Not Be Ignored
- To Command
- To Correct Others
- Keep Status Quo
- To Restrain
- Be Obeyed
- To Restrict
- To Hold Back

XI — BE NEEDED
- Improve Others
- Be Desired
- Need to Give
- Be a Critical Link
- Please
- Be Important
- Be Useful
- Affect Others
- To Rescue Others
- To fix others

XII — BE DUTIFUL
- Be Obligated
- Obey
- Prove Self
- Do the Right Thing
- Have a task
- Be Devoted
- Be a Follower
- Satisfy Others
- Have a Cause
- Please Others

XIII — BE FREE
- Be Unrestricted
- Be Independent
- Be Unobligated
- Be Privileged
- Be Autonomous
- Be Self Reliant
- Be Immune
- Be Sovereign
- Be Liberated
- Be a Rule Breaker
- Be Different

XIV — HONESTY
- Forthrightness
- Sincerity
- No Censoring
- Uprightness
- Loyalty
- No secrets
- No Lying
- Frankness
- Tell all
- Integrity

XV — ORDER
- Perfection
- Sequential
- Proper
- Symmetry
- Checklists
- To Resist Change
- Consistent
- Unvarying
- Regulated
- Sameness

XVI — PEACE
- Quietness
- Reconciliation
- Agreements
- Calmness
- Stillness
- Respite
- Unity
- Balance
- Steadiness
- Order

XVII — POWER
- Authority
- Omnipotence
- Stamina
- Capacity
- Strength
- Prerogative
- Results
- Might
- Influence

XVIII — RECOGNITION
- To Be Noticed
- To Be Regarded
- Well To Be
- Heeded
- Be Remembered
- Get Credit
- Be Seen
- Be Known for
- Be Acclaimed
- Be Taken Seriously
- Be Celebrated

XIX — SAFETY
- Security
- Fully Informed
- Cautious
- Protected
- Deliberate
- Be Alert
- Stable
- Be Vigilant
- Be Guarded

XX — WORK
- Force the outcome
- Make it happen
- Responsibility
- To Perform
- To be Industrious
- Work Hard
- Be Dedicated
- Task oriented
- Be Busy

XXI — OTHER
- Be Admired
- Be Up
- Be Positive
- Be Optimistic
- Be Spiritual
- Be of Service
- To Contribute
- To leave a Legacy
- To Have it All
- Be Good
- Happy

List of Possible Emotions

Primary emotion	Secondary emotion/feelings	Tertiary feelings/emotions
Love	Affection	Adoration, Fondness, Liking, Attractiveness, Caring
	Lust/Sexual desire	Arousal, Desire, Passion, Infatuation
	Longing	Longing
Joy	Cheerfulness	Amusement, Bliss, Gaiety, Glee, Jolliness, Joviality, Joy
	Zest	Enthusiasm, Zeal, Excitement, Thrill, Exhilaration
	Contentment	Pleasure
	Pride	Triumph
	Optimism	Eagerness, Hope
	Enthrallment	Enthrallment, Rapture
	Relief	Relief
Surprise	Surprise	Amazement, Astonishment
Anger	Irritability	Aggravation, Agitation, Annoyance, Grouchy, Grumpy
	Exasperation	Frustration
	Rage	Anger, Outrage, Fury, Wrath, Hostility, Ferocity, Bitterness
	Disgust	Revulsion, Contempt, Loathing
	Envy	Jealousy
	Torment	Torment
Sadness	Suffering	Agony, Anguish, Hurt
	Sadness	Depression, Despair, Gloom, Glumness, Unhappy, Grief
	Disappointment	Dismay, Displeasure
	Shame	Guilt, Regret, Remorse
	Neglect	Alienation, Defeatism, Dejection, Embarrassment, Homesick
	Sympathy	Pity
Fear	Horror	Alarm, Shock, Fear, Fright, Horror, Terror, Panic, Hysteria
	Nervousness	Anxiety, Suspense, Uneasiness, Apprehension, Worry